CMC Pasternak, Velvel
784 Jerusalem in Song
PAS

8717

JERUSALEM IN Song

COMPILED, EDITED AND ARRANGED
BY
VELVEL PASTERNAK

CURRICULUM COLLECTION
RATNER MEDIA CENTER
JEWISH EDUCATION CENTER
OF CLEVELAND
2030 South Taylor Road
Cleveland Heights, Ohio 44118

CEDARHURST, BALTIMORE, ISRAEL

Dedicated to the memory of
Rivka (Rhoda) Glickman
whose love for Jerusalem and Jewish music
was boundless

ISBN 0-933676-42-5

©1995 by Tara Publications
All rights reserved. No part of this book
may be reproduced in any form without
permission in writing from the publisher

Printed in the United States of America

CONTENTS

SONGS OF JERUSALEM

FROM THE BIBLE AND LITURGY

SONGS WITH PIANO ACCOMPANIMENT

CHORAL ARRANGEMENTS

KEY TO TRANSLITERATION

a .... as in c*a*r
ai .... as in s*i*gh
e .... as in f*e*d
e .... as in th*ey*
i .... as in p*i*n or m*e*
o .... as in f*o*rm or b*o*at
u .... as in tr*ue*
' .... as in *i*t
ch .... as in Ba*ch*

A song of steps by David:
I rejoiced when they said
"Let us go up to God's House"
Our feet would stand
Within your gates, O Jerusalem
Jerusalem is built
Like a city that is bound together.
For it is there that the tribes ascend
The tribes of God
A testimony to Israel
To praise the name of God
For it is there that thrones of justice are set
Thrones of the house of David
Seek peace for Jerusalem
May those who love you prosper
Peace be within your ramparts
Prosperity in your palaces
For the sake of my brothers and friends
I say, "Peace be within you"
For the sake of the House of the Lord our God
I will seek your good

Psalm 122

FOREWORD

This collection, by no means exhaustive, has been conceived as an overview of songs pertaining to Jerusalem. The prayer for the return to Jerusalem is recited by Jews in the *Amidah* (the silent devotion) three times daily and the city has been the focus of Judaism since the destruction of the Temple. We hope that this volume dedicated to the three thousand anniversary of Jerusalem will become a repertoire of songs to be enjoyed by individuals, families, schools, camps and Jewish Center educators. The selections found in the four sections of this collection will provide the Jewish music lover with a broad panorama of material heretofore unavailable in a single edition. A functional transliteration scheme has been used and it is consistent with that employed in other Tara publications. Every effort has been made to clear and give proper credit to the copyright holders. In a number of cases copyright search has proved fruitless and the songs have been credited as folk songs.

ACKNOWLEDGMENTS

Grateful appreciation is extended to: my colleague, Seymour Silbermintz, noted musician and educator, for his painstaking proofreading of this manuscript and for the suggestions, both musical and textual; my son, Gedalia, who was always available to assist with his technical expertise; my daughter, Shira Be'eri, for her invaluable criticism and suggestions; my son Mayer, who by running the daily operations of Tara Publications, has enabled me to continue research and product development. ACUM Ltd. Israel, for the reprint rights to the songs of Israeli composers; Goldie, my life-long partner, who is not only patient with a sometimes impatient transcriber and editor but is also an able assistant in his often arduous labor in the vineyard of Jewish music.

SONGS OF JERUSALEM

TEMPLE FACADE - HOLYLAND HOTEL

Lach Y'rushalayim

Music: E. Rubinstein
Lyrics: A. Etinger

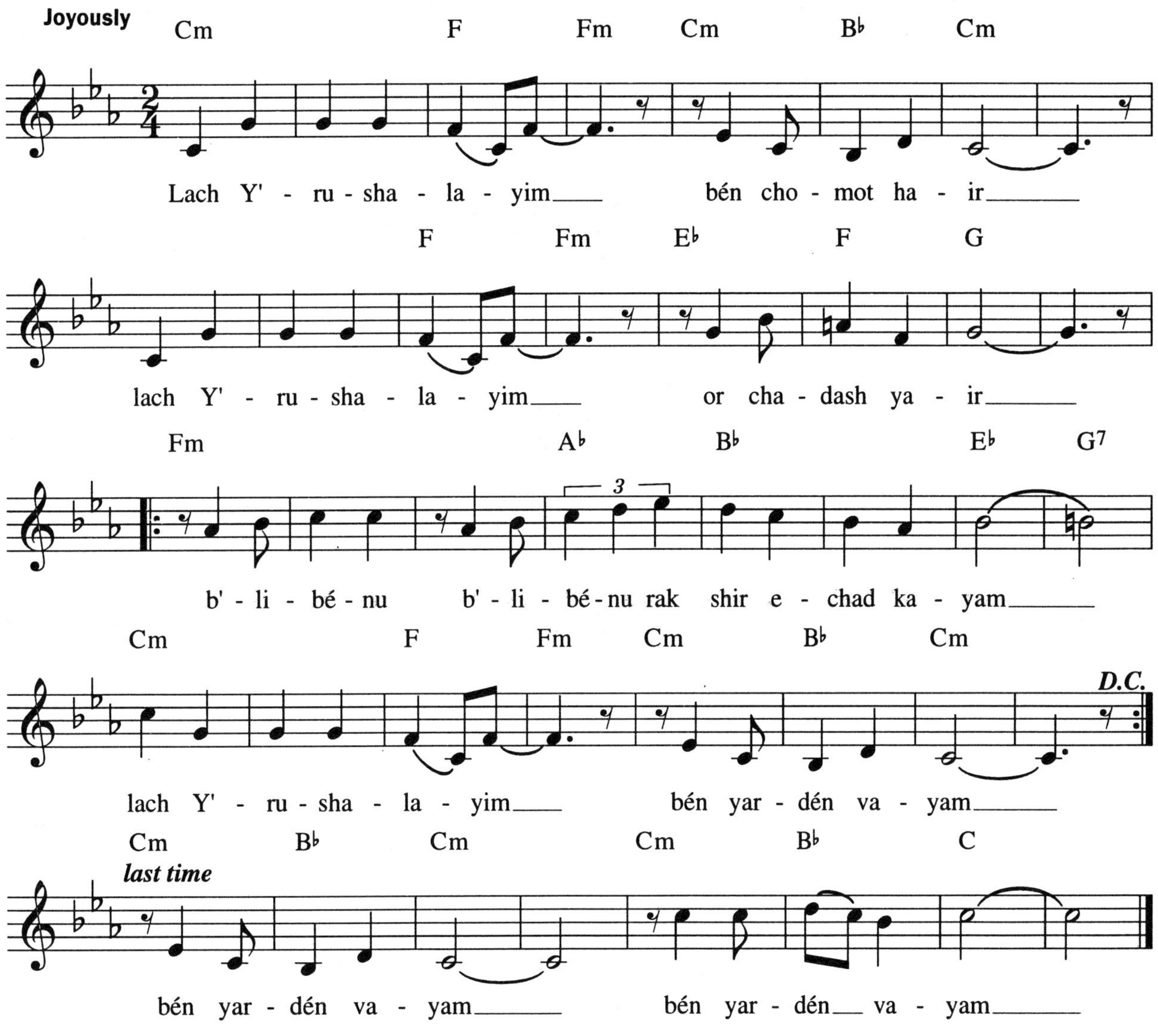

Joyously

Cm F Fm Cm B♭ Cm
Lach Y' - ru - sha - la - yim___ bén cho - mot ha - ir___

F Fm E♭ F G
lach Y' - ru - sha - la - yim___ or cha - dash ya - ir___

Fm A♭ B♭ E♭ G7
b' - li - bé - nu b' - li - bé - nu rak shir e - chad ka - yam___

Cm F Fm Cm B♭ Cm *D.C.*
lach Y' - ru - sha - la - yim___ bén yar - dén va - yam___

Cm B♭ Cm Cm B♭ C
last time
bén yar - dén va - yam___ bén yar - dén___ va - yam___

© Edition Paamonim

Lach Y'-ru-shala-yim bén cho-mot ha-ir		לָךְ יְרוּשָׁלַיִם בֵּין חוֹמוֹת הָעִיר
Lach Y'-ru-sha-la-yim or cha-dash ya-ir		לָךְ יְרוּשָׁלַיִם אוֹר חָדָשׁ יָאִיר
Refrain		*פזמון*
B'-li-bé-nu rak shir e-chad ka-yam		בְּלִבֵּנוּ רַק שִׁיר אֶחָד קַיָּם
Lach Y'-ru-sha-la-yim bén Yar-dén va-yam		לָךְ יְרוּשָׁלַיִם בֵּין יַרְדֵּן וָיָם
Lach Y'-ru-sha-la-yim lach k'-du-mim va-hod		לָךְ יְרוּשָׁלַיִם לָךְ קְדוּמִים וָהוֹד
Lach Y'-ru-sha-la-yim lach ra-zim va-sod	Refrain	לָךְ יְרוּשָׁלַיִם לָךְ רָזִים וָסוֹד *פזמון*
Lach Y'-ru-sha-la-yim shir ni-sa ta-mid		לָךְ יְרוּשָׁלַיִם שִׁיר נִישָּׂא תָּמִיד
Lach Y'-ru-sha-la-yim ir mig-dal Da-vid	Refrain	לָךְ יְרוּשָׁלַיִם עִיר מִגְדַּל דָּוִד *פזמון*

For you, O Jerusalem, fortress of David, let a new light shine. In our hearts there exists but one song, a song dedicated to you.

Zot Y'rushalayim

Music: N. Heiman
Lyrics: E. Peretz

Moderately

Dm Gm
Ga - got shel bin - ya - nim v' - e - ven m' - su - te - tet

A A7 Dm F C
u - var - cho - vot hem - yat shal - va kmu - sa u - ma sha - vim ra - a - na -

F Am/E F Dm Gm A
nim tsa - me - ret m' - ra - te - tet u - ts'chok ba - cha - tsé - rot bé - not chav - lé kvi -

Dm D A Dm
sa zot Y' - ru - sha - la - yim shel av - né ha - cho - shen

D Gm C F A B♭
zot Y' - ru - sha - la - yim hab - nu - ya l' - tal - pi - ot zot Y' - ru - sha - la - yim

C F Gm C7 F Gm/E A7 Dm
shel av - nei ha - cho - shen zot Y' - ru - sha - la - yim hab - nu - ya l' - tal - pi - ot

© NMC Music

Ga-got shel bin-ya-nim v'-e-ven m'-su-te-tet
U-vir-cho-vot hem-yat shal-va k'-mu-sa
U-ma-sha-vim ra-a-na-nim tsa-me-ret m'-ra-te-tet
U-ts'-chok ba-cha-tsé-rot bé-not chav-lé k'-vi-sa
Refrain
Zot Y'-ru-sha-la-yim shel av-né ha-cho-shen
Zot Y'-ru-sha-la-yim hab-nu-ya l'-tal-pi-ot

גַּגּוֹת שֶׁל בִּנְיָנִים וְאֶבֶן מְסֻתֶּתֶת
וּבָרְחוֹבוֹת הֶמְיַת שַׁלְוָה כְּמוּסָה
וּמַשָּׁבִים רַעֲנַנִּים צַמֶּרֶת מְרַטֶּטֶת
וּצְחוֹק בַּחֲצֵרוֹת בֵּינוֹת חַבְלֵי כְּבִיסָה
פזמון
זֹאת יְרוּשָׁלַיִם שֶׁל אַבְנֵי הַחֹשֶׁן
זֹאת יְרוּשָׁלַיִם הַבְּנוּיָה לְתַלְפִּיּוֹת

Mé-a la sh'-a-rim s'-vi-va a-tsé ha-za-yit
Ba-sim-ta-ot zar-ka k'var ha-sé-va
U-mit-nag-nim ha-miz-mo-rim
Mé-é-ver har ha-ba-yit
Ba-de-rech ha-yo-re-det el ha-mats-lé-va Refrain

מֵאָה לָהּ שְׁעָרִים סְבִיבָהּ עֲצֵי הַזַּיִת
בַּסִּמְטָאוֹת זָרְקָה כְּבָר הַשֵּׂיבָה
וּמִתְנַגְּנִים הַמִּזְמוֹרִים
מֵעֵבֶר הַר הַבַּיִת
בַּדֶּרֶךְ הַיּוֹרֶדֶת אֶל הַמַּצְלֵבָה *פזמון*

V'-kol ha-mu-a-zin o-le hats-ri-ach
Mich-né-si-yot o-nim pa-a-mo-nim
V'-na-ar kat im hat-fi-lin
Et t'-fi-lat shu-té-ach
U-mit-maz-nim mé-al ha-ir ha-ni-gu-nim Refrain

וְקוֹל הַמּוּאַזִּין עוֹלֶה הַצְּרִיחַ
מִכְּנֵסִיּוֹת עוֹנִים פַּעֲמוֹנִים
וְנַעַר קָט עִם הַתְּפִלִּין
אֶת תְּפִלָּת שׁוֹטֵחַ
וּמִתְמַזְּגִים מֵעַל הָעִיר הַנִּגּוּנִים *פזמון*

In the streets there is the hum of secret tranquillity. This is Jerusalem of the stones of the Western Wall. This is Jerusalem magnificently built.

Any one who prays in Jerusalem—it is as if he prays before the throne of glory. For the gates of heaven are there and the entrance is open to hear.

Pirkei D'Rebbe Eliezer 35

Jerusalem Of Earth And Sky

Music: I. Antelis
Lyrics: D. Grossman/E. R. Grossman

Lyrically

G C D7 Bm7 Em7
Heav-ens home e - ter - nal place Je - ru - sa - lem a - bove re -

Am D7 G C D7
flect - ions of my dream for us a home of cob - ble stones that's built on bit - ter

Bm7 Em7 Am D7 G
tears and dream a - bout Je - ru - sa - lem ___ Earth - ly home oh mor - tal
Prayer - ful home en - vis - ioned

C D7 Bm7 Em7 Am D7
place Je - ru - sa - lem of man re - flect - ions of my dream
space Je - ru - sa - lem I see earth and sky a u - ni - ty

G C D7 Bm7 Em7
for us a home of mys - tic dreams that's built on an - gel wings and
for us a hope of sha - lom a true re - a - li - ty and

Am D7 C D Bm Em
dream a - bout Je - ru - sa - lem of earth and of the sky ___
live a - gain Je - ru - sa - lem of earth and of the sky ___

Am D G G7 C D
In the cen - ter stands a wall the ci - ty's soul whose stones do

Bm Em Am Am-5 G/D D7
cry ___ Je - ru - sa - lem shall live and ne - ver

1. G C D7 Bm7 Em7 Am D7 2. G
die die Je - ru - sa - lem shall

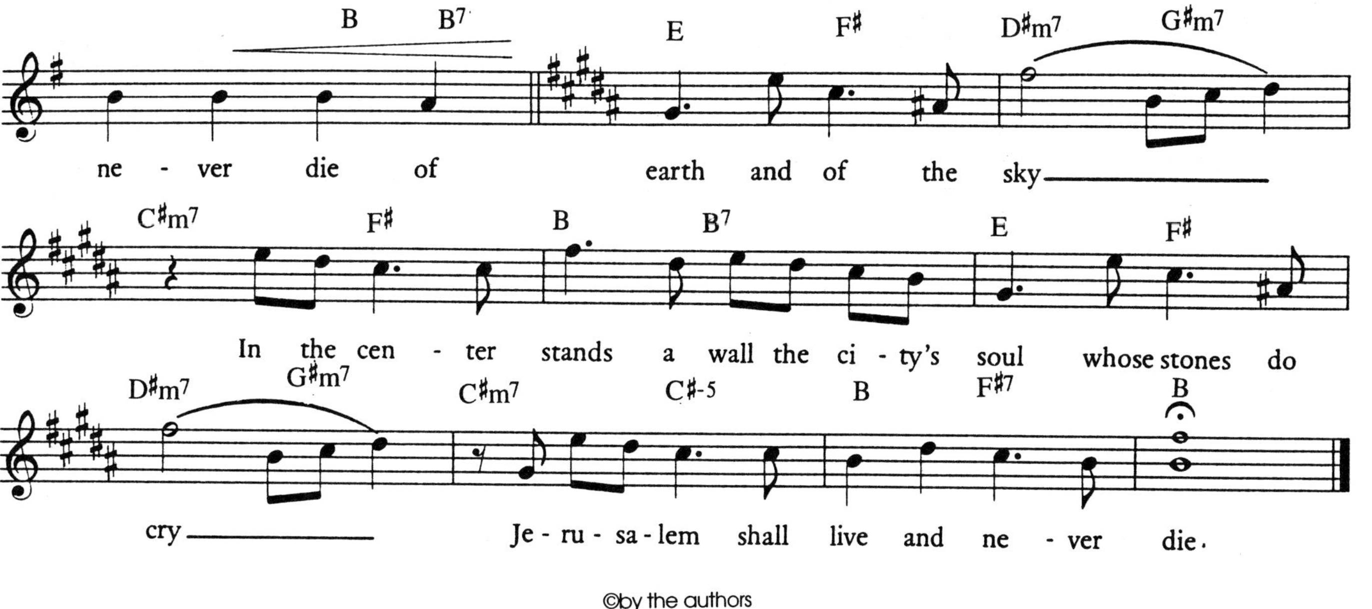

©by the authors

Heaven's home eternal place
Jerusalem above
Reflections of my dream
For us a home of cobblestones
That's built on bitter tears
And dream about Jerusalem.

Earthly home, oh mortal place
Jerusalem of man
Reflections of my dream
For us a home of mystic dream
That's built on angel wings
And dream about Jerusalem
Of earth and of sky

At the center stands a wall
The city's soul whose stones do cry
Jerusalem shall live and never die.

Prayerful home, envisioned space,
Jerusalem, I see earth and sky a unity
For us a home of *shalom*, a true reality
And live again Jerusalem
Of earth and of the sky.

Ani Ole Lirushalayim

Music: Y. Hadar
Lyrics: A. Rachman

Moderately

Dm A
A - ni o - le li - ru - sha - la - yim___ u - lai ba - nu et ha - mik - dash_

A7 Dm
_____ a - ni no - sé al ha - k'té - fa - yim___ ka - dé ziv - da cha - lav u - d'vash_

D D7 Gm
_____ a - ni o - le l' - ir ha - ko - desh___ la - ga - at b' - chi - sé Sh'lo - mo_

Gm Dm B♭ Gm6 A7
_____ a - ni pa - shut ro - tse la - da - at___ im chai mal - ki u - ma sh'lo - mo_

D7 Gm C7 F
_____ a - ni o - le li - ru - sha - la - yim___ a - ni o - le l' - ir Da - vid_

B♭ Gm A7
_________ a - ni o - le l' - har ha - ba - yit___ she - li ha -

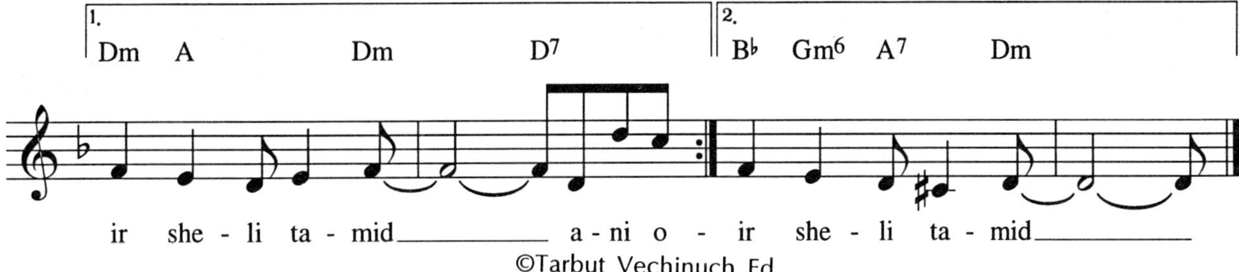

©Tarbut Vechinuch Ed.

A-ni o-le li-ru-sha-la-yim u-lai ba-nu et ha-mik-dash	אֲנִי עוֹלֶה לִירוּשָׁלַיִם אוּלַי בָּנוּ אֶת הַמִּקְדָּשׁ
A-ni no-sé al ha-k'-té-fa-yim ka-dé ziv-da cha-lav u-d'-vash	אֲנִי נוֹשֵׂא עַל הַכְּתֵפַיִם כַּדֵּי זִבְדָה חָלָב וּדְבַשׁ
A-ni o-le l'-ir ha-ko-desh la-ga-at b'-chi-sé Sh'-lo-mo	אֲנִי עוֹלֶה לְעִיר הַקֹּדֶשׁ לָגַעַת בְּכִסֵּא שְׁלֹמֹה
A-ni pa-shut ro-tse la-da-at im chai mal-ki u-ma sh'-lo-mo	אֲנִי פָּשׁוּט רוֹצֶה לָדַעַת אִם חַי מַלְכִּי וּמַה שְּׁלֹמוֹ
Refrain	פזמון
A-ni o-le li-ru-sha-la-yim a-ni o-le l'-ir Da-vid	אֲנִי עוֹלֶה לִירוּשָׁלַיִם אֲנִי עוֹלֶה לְעִיר דָּוִד
A-ni o-le l'-har ha-ba-yit she-li ha-ir she-li ta-mid	אֲנִי עוֹלֶה לְהַר הַבַּיִת שֶׁלִּי הָעִיר שֶׁלִּי תָּמִיד
A-ni o-le li-ru-sha-la-yim za-nach-ti é-der v'-cha-lil	אֲנִי עוֹלֶה לִירוּשָׁלַיִם זָנַחְתִּי עֵדֶר וְחָלִיל
A-ni no-sé al hak-té-fa-yim t'-le u-g'-di mé-ha-ga-lil	אֲנִי נוֹשֵׂא עַל הַכְּתֵפַיִם טָלֶה וּגְדִי מֵהַגָּלִיל
A-ni o-le l'-ir ha-né-tsach ho-léch li b'-ik-vot ha-or	אֲנִי עוֹלֶה לְעִיר הַנֵּצַח הוֹלֵךְ לִי בְּעִקְבוֹת הָאוֹר
Lish-mo-a im Da-vid ha-me-lech od m'-na-gén al ha-ki-nor	לִשְׁמוֹעַ אִם דָּוִד הַמֶּלֶךְ עוֹד מְנַגֵּן עַל הַכִּנּוֹר
A-ni o-le li-ru-sha-la-yim u-mé-ra-chok kol u-ga-vim	אֲנִי עוֹלֶה לִירוּשָׁלַיִם וּמֵרָחוֹק קוֹל עֻגָבִים
A-ni no-sé al hak-té-fa-yim esh-kol ma-tok shel a-na-vim	אֲנִי נוֹשֵׂא עַל הַכְּתֵפַיִם אֶשְׁכּוֹל מָתוֹק שֶׁל עֲנָבִים
A-ni o-le l'-ir E-lo-ha a-ni sho-mé-a shir cha-dash	אֲנִי עוֹלֶה לְעִיר אֱלוֹהַּ אֲנִי שׁוֹמֵעַ שִׁיר חָדָשׁ
U-lai chaz-ru k'-var ha-l'-vi-im u-m'-nag-nim sham ba-mik-dash	אוּלַי חָזְרוּ כְּבָר הַלְוִיִּים וּמְנַגְּנִים שָׁם בַּמִּקְדָּשׁ

I travel to Jerusalem-perhaps the Temple has been rebuilt. I travel to Jerusalem-perhaps I shall hear David play on his lyre.

Ani Ole Lirushalayim II

Music: C. Parchi
Lyrics: A. Rachman

Allegro moderato

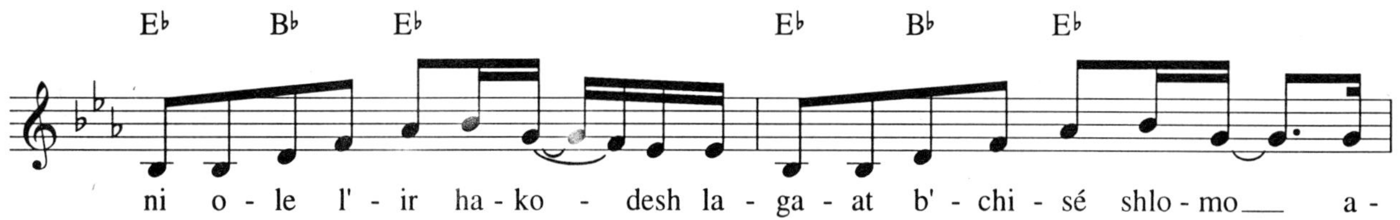

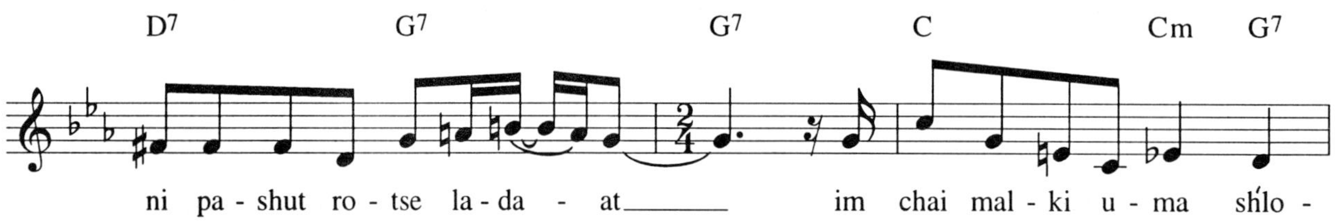

© by the authors

A-ni o-le li-ru-sha-la-yim u-lai ba-nu et ha-mik-dash	אֲנִי עוֹלֶה לִירוּשָׁלַיִם אוּלַי בָּנוּ אֶת הַמִּקְדָּשׁ
A-ni no-sé al ha-k'-té-fa-yim ka-dé ziv-da cha-lav u-d'-vash	אֲנִי נוֹשֵׂא עַל הַכְּתֵפַיִם כַּדֵּי זִבְדָּה חָלָב וּדְבַשׁ
A-ni o-le l'-ir ha-ko-desh la-ga-at b'-chi-sé Sh'-lo-mo	אֲנִי עוֹלֶה לְעִיר הַקֹּדֶשׁ לָגַעַת בְּכִסֵּא שְׁלֹמֹה
A-ni pa-shut ro-tse la-da-at im chai mal-ki u-ma sh'-lo-mo	אֲנִי פָּשׁוּט רוֹצֶה לָדַעַת אִם חַי מַלְכִּי וּמָה שְׁלֹמוֹ
Refrain	פזמון
A-ni o-le li-ru-sha-la-yim a-ni o-le l'-ir Da-vid	אֲנִי עוֹלֶה לִירוּשָׁלַיִם אֲנִי עוֹלֶה לְעִיר דָּוִד
A-ni o-le l'-har ha-ba-yit she-li ha-ir she-li ta-mid	אֲנִי עוֹלֶה לְהַר הַבַּיִת שֶׁלִּי הָעִיר שֶׁלִּי תָּמִיד

A-ni o-le li-ru-sha-la-yim za-nach-ti é-der v'-cha-lil	אֲנִי עוֹלֶה לִירוּשָׁלַיִם זָנַחְתִּי עֵדֶר וְחָלִיל
A-ni no-sé al hak-té-fa-yim t'-le u-g'-di mé-ha-ga-lil	אֲנִי נוֹשֵׂא עַל הַכְּתֵפַיִם טְלֶה וּגְדִי מֵהַגָּלִיל
A-ni o-le l'-ir ha-né-tsach ho-léch li b'-ik-vot ha-or	אֲנִי עוֹלֶה לְעִיר הַנֵּצַח הוֹלֵךְ לִי בְּעִקְבוֹת הָאוֹר
Lish-mo-a im Da-vid ha-me-lech od m'-na-gén al ha-ki-nor	לִשְׁמוֹעַ אִם דָּוִד הַמֶּלֶךְ עוֹד מְנַגֵּן עַל הַכִּנּוֹר

A-ni o-le li-ru-sha-la-yim u-mé-ra-chok kol u-ga-vim	אֲנִי עוֹלֶה לִירוּשָׁלַיִם וּמֵרָחוֹק קוֹל עֻגָבִים
A-ni no-sé al hak-té-fa-yim esh-kol ma-tok shel a-na-vim	אֲנִי נוֹשֵׂא עַל הַכְּתֵפַיִם אֶשְׁכּוֹל מָתוֹק שֶׁל עֲנָבִים
A-ni o-le l'-ir E-lo-ha a-ni sho-mé-a shir cha-dash	אֲנִי עוֹלֶה לְעִיר אֱלוֹהַּ אֲנִי שׁוֹמֵעַ שִׁיר חָדָשׁ
U-lai chaz-ru k'-var ha-l'-vi-im u-m'-nag-nim sham ba-mik-dash	אוּלַי חָזְרוּ כְּבָר הַלְוִיִּם וּמְנַגְּנִים שָׁם בַּמִּקְדָּשׁ

I travel to Jerusalem-perhaps the Temple has been rebuilt. I travel to Jerusalem-perhaps I shall hear David play on his lyre.

From the day that Jerusalem and the Temple were destroyed, there is no happiness before the Holy One, blessed be He. So it will be until Jerusalem will be rebuilt and Israel will return to its midst....

Yalkut Shimoni Eicha

Jerusalem Is Mine

Music: K. Karen

Lyrically

C F C F C F G C Am F C /E G Am Em/G Dm/F

I am the sun Je - ru - sa - lem___ you are a paint - ed
or - chard in the sand___ I am the fruit you

C/E F G F/C G/B C G/B Am F Dm/C F/A Em/G Dm/F C/E Dm7 Dm7/A G

sky___ I am a bird Je - ru - sal - lem___ you have the wings to
bear___ you are the glove that warms my hands___ I am the smile you

G/C C G/C C G/B F/A B/A Em/G A/G D/F♯ D D/C Bm Em F Em D4 G C

fly you are the fa - ther of my dream___ I am the gift of
wear you are the mu - sic of the hills___ I am the words that

F B♭/F F C/E Dm Am/C B♭ Am G C F G C G6/B Am F C/E G

time I am your child Je - ru - sa - lem___ Je - ru - sa - lem___ is
rhyme I am your song Je - ru - sa - lem___ Je - ru - sa - lem___ is

1. Am Em/G Dm/F C/E Dm | 2. C/E F B♭ F C G B♭ F C G F/G

mine You are the | mine You are the cra - dle of free - dom

G/C C G/C C G C G C F G/F F C/E Dm Am/C B♭ F/A G4 C

I am the har - vest of Spring - time You are the dawn of a new day

© by the author

I am the sun Jerusalem, you are a painted sky
I am a bird Jerusalem, you have the wings to fly
You are the father of my dream, I am the gift of time
I am your child Jerusalem, Jerusalem is mine
You are the orchard in the sand, I am the fruit you bear
You are the glove that warms my hand, I am the smile you wear
You are the music of the hills, I am the words that rhyme
I am your song Jerusalem, Jerusalem is mine
You are the cradle of freedom, you are the harvest of Springtime
You are the dawn of a new day, I am tomorrow, you are forever
You are my shelter from the storm, I am your guiding light
You are a book whose leaves are torn, I am the page you write
You are the branches of a tree, I am a clinging vine
I am a prayer Jerusalem, Jerusalem is mine
I have come home Jerusalem, Jerusalem is mine.

Y'rushalayim Ir Hakodesh

Music: Folk
Lyrics: E. Harussi

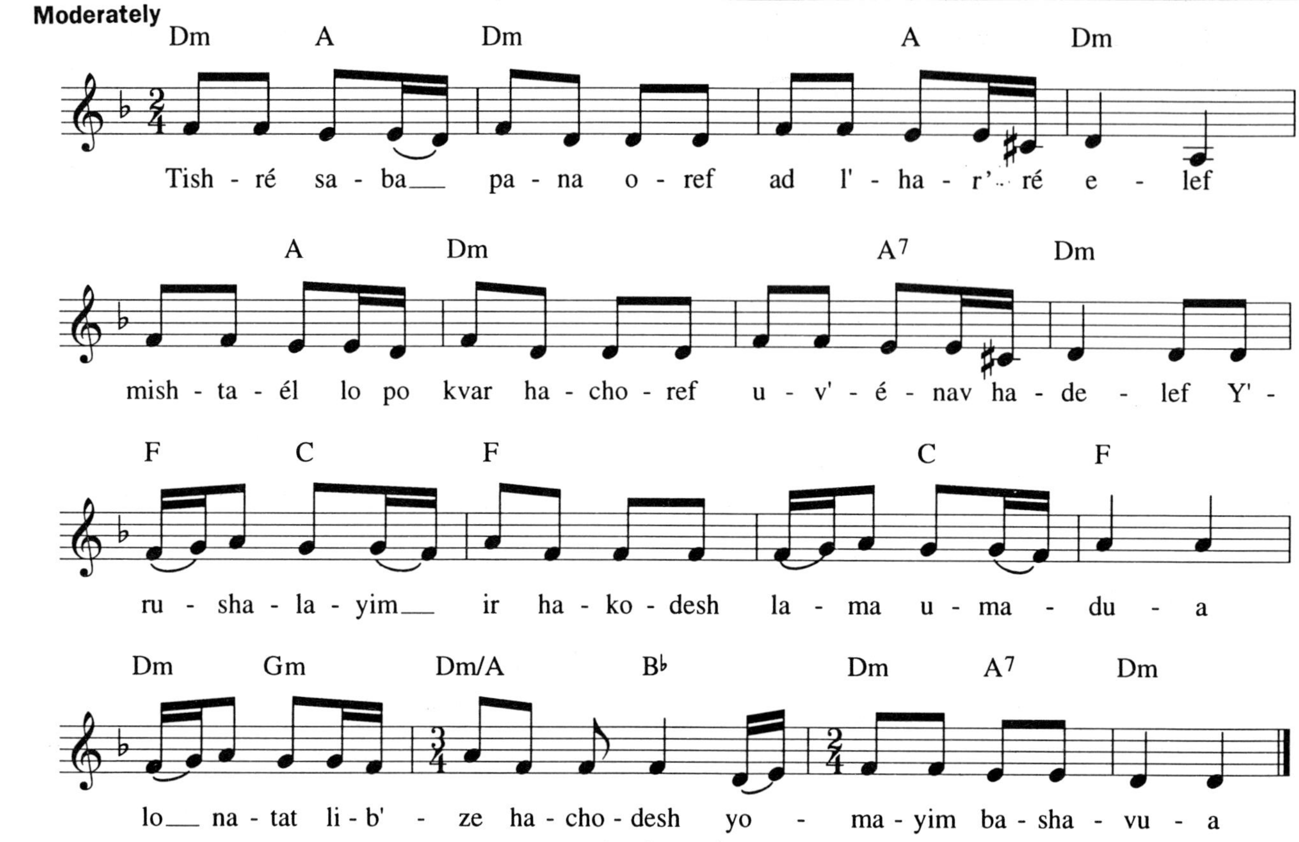

Moderately

Dm A Dm A Dm
Tish - ré sa - ba pa - na o - ref ad l' - ha - r' - ré e - lef

A Dm A7 Dm
mish - ta - él lo po kvar ha - cho - ref u - v' - é - nav ha - de - lef Y' -

F C F C F
ru - sha - la - yim ir ha - ko - desh la - ma u - ma - du - a

Dm Gm Dm/A B♭ Dm A7 Dm
lo na - tat li - b' - ze ha - cho - desh yo - ma - yim ba - sha - vu - a

©by the author

Tish-ré sa-ba pa-na o-réf
Ad l'-ha-r'-ré e-lef
Mish-ta-él lo po kvar ha-cho-ref
U-v'-é-nav ha-de-lef
Refrain
Y'-ru-sha-la-yim ir ha-ko-desh
La-ma u-ma-du-a
Lo na-tat li b'-ze ha-cho-desh
Yo-ma-yim ba-sha-vu-a

תִּשְׁרֵי סַבָּא פָּנָה עֹרֶף
עַד לְהָרְרֵי אֶלֶף
מִשְׁתָּעֵל לוֹ פֹּה כְּבָר הַחֹרֶף
וּבְעֵינָיו הַדֶּלֶף
פזמון
יְרוּשָׁלַיִם עִיר הַקֹּדֶשׁ
לָמָּה וּמַדּוּעַ
לֹא נָתַתְּ לִי בְּזֶה הַחֹדֶשׁ
יוֹמַיִם בַּשָּׁבוּעַ

U-va-tsrif bo-che ha-ye-led
Tsom-chot lo shi-na-yim
Gal-mud hu y'-chi-di ba-che-led
Ki ho-rim lo a-yin Refrain

וּבַצְּרִיף בּוֹכֶה הַיֶּלֶד
צוֹמְחוֹת לוֹ שִׁנַּיִם
גַּלְמוּד הוּא יְחִידִי בַּחֶלֶד
כִּי הוֹרִים לוֹ אַיִן *פזמון*

Ba-mach-tsa-va na-fal a-vi-cha
Nish-ma-to ba-to-hu
Én da-var s'-gor et pi-cha
Ti-ye cho-tsév ka-mo-hu Refrain

בַּמַּחְצָבָה נָפַל אָבִיךָ
נִשְׁמָתוֹ בַּתֹּהוּ
אֵין דָּבָר סְגוֹר אֶת פִּיךָ
תִּהְיֶה חוֹצֵב כָּמוֹהוּ *פזמון*

The month of Tishré is long gone and the winter with its dripping rain is here. Jerusalem, holy city could you not give me two days work a week?

Shiro Shel Aba

N. Shemer

Rhythmically

Dm C F C7 F A7
Im ba - har cha - tsav - ta e - ven l' - ha - kim bin - yan cha - dash

Dm C F C
ba - har cha - tsav - ta e - ven l' - ha - kim bin - yan cha - dash

B♭ F Gm A
lo la - shav a - chi cha - tsav - ta l' - vin - yan cha - dash ki

B♭ F Gm A7 Dm
min ha - a - va - nim ha - é - le yi - ba - ne ha - mik - dash

Dm Gm Dm A7 Dm
yi - ba - ne yi - ba - ne yi - ba - ne ha - mik - dash yi - ba - ne yi - ba - ne

1. Gm Dm
yi - ba - ne ha - mik - dash

2. Gm A7 Dm
yi - ba - ne ha - mik - dash

© by the author

Im ba-har cha-tsav-ta e-ven l'-ha-kim bin-yàn cha-dash
Ba-har cha-tsav-ta e-ven l'-ha-kim bin-yan cha-dash
Lo la-shav a-chi cha-tsav-ta l'-vin-yan cha-dash
Ki min ha-a-va-nim ha-é-lu yi-ba-ne ha-mik-dash
Yi-ba-ne ha-mik-dash

אִם בָּהָר חָצַבְתָּ אֶבֶן לְהָקִים בִּנְיָן חָדָשׁ
בָּהָר חָצַבְתָּ אֶבֶן לְהָקִים בִּנְיָן חָדָשׁ
לֹא לַשָּׁוְא אָחִי חָצַבְתָּ לְבִנְיָן חָדָשׁ
כִּי מִן הָאֲבָנִים הָאֵלּוּ
יִבָּנֶה הַמִּקְדָּשׁ

If you have cleared stones upon the mountain to build a new home, then your work, my brother, has not been in vain. From just such work the Temple will be rebuilt.

Additional text page 187

Agadat Shalom Shabazi

Music: Y. Badichi
Lyrics: U. Barzilai

Moderately

F F6 Gm7
Mi - yom ri - shon ad yom shi - shi ba - tso - ho - ra - yim

C7 Gm7 C7 Gm7 C7 F
yo - shév ra - bi sha - lom sha - ba - zi ba - cha - nut

Dm C B♭ F
o - rég hu v' - to - ve go - zér b' - mis - pa - ra - yim

C Gm7 C F6 C7 F
o - hév et ha - m'la - cha v' - so - né ra - ba - nut

F C F F
bén ha - ar - ba - yim al har ha -

Gm C7
ba - yit ba la - t'fi - la bi - ru - sha -

1. F | 2. F C7 F
la - yim la - yim

©by the authors

Mi-yom ri-shon ad yom shi-shi ba-tso-ho-ra-yim
Yo-shév Rabi Shalom Shabazi ba-cha-nut
O-rég hu v'-to-ve go-zér b'-mis-pa-ra-yim
O-hév et ha-m'la-cha v'-so-né ra-ba-nut
Refrain
Bén ha-ar-ba-yim al har ha-ba-yit
Ba la-t'fi-la bi-ru-sha-la-yim

מִיּוֹם רִאשׁוֹן עַד יוֹם שִׁשִּׁי בַּצָּהֳרַיִם
יוֹשֵׁב רַבִּי שָׁלוֹם שַׁבָּזִי בַּחֲנוּת
אוֹרֵג הוּא וְטוֹוֶה גּוֹזֵר בְּמִסְפָּרַיִם
אוֹהֵב אֶת הַמְּלָאכָה וְשׂוֹנֵא רַבָּנוּת
פזמון
בֵּין הָעַרְבַּיִם עַל הַר הַבַּיִת
בָּא לַתְּפִלָּה בִּירוּשָׁלַיִם

Kol yom v'-yom mé-hash-ki-a v'-chol
O-chéz Rabi Shalom Shabazi b'-é-to
Mi-ba-ad cha-lo-no nir-ét Y'-ru-sha-la-yim
Az k'-ésh o-la bo-ka-at shi-ra-to Refrain

כָּל יוֹם וְיוֹם מֵהַשְׁקִיעָה וְכָל
אוֹחֵז רַבִּי שָׁלוֹם שַׁבָּזִי בְּעֵטוֹ
מִבַּעַד חַלּוֹנוֹ נִרְאֵית יְרוּשָׁלַיִם
אָז כְּאֵשׁ עוֹלָה בּוֹקַעַת שִׁירָתוֹ *פזמון*

Mi-yom shi-shi ad yom ri-shon mi-dé sha-vu-a
O-zév Rabi Shalom Shabazi et ha-ir
K'-mo b'-chol Sha-bat hu tas al k'naf ha-ru-ach
La-ko-tel she-sa-rad b'-ir Da-vid Refrain

מִיּוֹם שִׁשִּׁי עַד יוֹם רִאשׁוֹן מִדֵּי שָׁבוּעַ
עוֹזֵב רַבִּי שָׁלוֹם שַׁבָּזִי אֶת הָעִיר
כְּמוֹ בְּכָל שַׁבָּת הוּא טָס עַל כְּנַף הָרוּחַ
לַכֹּתֶל שֶׁשָּׂרַד בְּעִיר דָּוִד *פזמון*

Mi-yom ri-shon ad yom shi-shi ba-tso-ho-ra-yim
Cho-zér Rabi Shalom Shabazi la-t'fi-ra
B'-i-sho-nav yésh or, ze or Y'-ru-sha-la-yim
A-sher da-vak b'-chol ha-ba b'-sha-a-ra Refrain

מִיּוֹם רִאשׁוֹן עַד יוֹם שִׁשִּׁי בַּצָּהֳרַיִם
חוֹזֵר רַבִּי שָׁלוֹם שַׁבָּזִי לַתְּפִירָה
בְּאִישׁוֹנָיו יֵשׁ אוֹר זֶה אוֹר יְרוּשָׁלַיִם
אֲשֶׁר דָּבֵק בְּכָל הַבָּא בְּשַׁעֲרָה

Rabbi Shalom Shabazi works all week long. On Friday night he comes to pray in Jerusalem on the Temple Mount. Every Sabbath he flies on the wings of the wind to the Western Wall which survived in the City of David.

AT PRAYER

T'fila Lirushalayim

S. Paikov

Allegro moderato

Em B Am B
Y' - ru - sha - la - yim é - né kol Yis - ra - él é -

Em C G D G D
la - yich n' - su - ot u - vit - chi - na Y' - ru - sha - la - yim Y' -

B7 Em C B7 1. Em D
ru - sha - la - yim har - shi - ni l' - za - mér lach tfi - la Y' -

2. Em Am B7 Em Am D7 G 1. C G
la Y' - ru - sha - la - yim Y' - ru - sha - la - yim hit - pa - l' - li lish - lo - mé - nu l' -

Am D7 G Em 2. C G Am B B7 Em
shlom kol Yis - ra - él Y' - pa - l' - li lish - lo - mé - nu lish - lom kol Yis - ra - él

©by NMC Music

Y'-ru-sha-la-yim é-né kol Yis-ra-él	יְרוּשָׁלַיִם עֵינֵי כָּל יִשְׂרָאֵל
É-la-yich n'-su-ot u-vit-chi-na	אֵלַיִךְ נְשׂוּאוֹת וּבִתְחִנָּה
Y'-ru-sha-la-yim ,Y'-ru-sha-la-yim	יְרוּשָׁלַיִם, יְרוּשָׁלַיִם
Har-shi-ni l'-za-mér lach t'-fi-la	הַרְשִׁינִי לְזַמֵּר לָךְ תְּפִלָּה
Refrain	פזמון
Y'-ru-sha-la-yim ,Y'-ru-sha-la-yim	יְרוּשָׁלַיִם, יְרוּשָׁלַיִם
Hit-pa-l'-li lish-lo-mé-nu	הִתְפַּלְלִי לִשְׁלוֹמֵנוּ
Lish-lom kol Yis-ra-él	לִשְׁלוֹם כָּל יִשְׂרָאֵל
Y'-ru-sha-la-yim k'-ye-led ez-k'-réch	יְרוּשָׁלַיִם כְּיֶלֶד אֶזְכְּרֵךְ
Éch a-ba b'-ta-lit o-tach bé-réch	אֵיךְ אַבָּא בְּטַלִּית אוֹתָךְ בֵּרֵךְ
Mé-az har-bé sha-nim	מֵאָז הַרְבֵּה שָׁנִים
Cha-lam-ti bén al-fé a-chim	חָלַמְתִּי בֵּין אַלְפֵי אַחִים
La-yom she-bo a-shuv lir-o-téch Refrain	לַיּוֹם שֶׁבּוֹ אָשׁוּב לִרְאוֹתֵךְ פזמון
Y'-ru-sha-la-yim miv-tsar kol ha-m'la-chim	יְרוּשָׁלַיִם מִבְצַר כָּל הַמְּלָכִים
Hé-chan hém ya-fa-ti ha-n'-vi-im	הֵיכָן הֵם יָפָתֵי הַנְּבִיאִים
Ha-im yish-ma-u	הַאִם יִשְׁמְעוּ
Siv-lot a-mi yé-da-u	סִבְלוֹת עַמִּי יֵדְעוּ
Mi y'-kab-tsém mi-bén ha-go-yim?	מִי יְקַבְּצֵם מִבֵּין הַגּוֹיִם?

Oh, Jerusalem! The eyes of all Israel are turned towards you in supplication. Jerusalem, let me sing for you-a prayer. Jerusalem, pray for us for peace for all of Israel. I remember you when I was young, how father in his prayer shawl blessed you. And ever since, along with thousands of my brethren I have been dreaming of the day when I would see you again. Fortress of kings, where have all your prophets gone? Do they hear? Do they know the suffering of my people? Who shall gather the dispersed among the nations?

> There is no love like the love
> of Torah
> There is no wisdom like the
> wisdom of the land of Israel
> There is no beauty like the
> beauty of Jerusalem
>
> Avot D'rabi Natan

Y'rushalayim Ha'acheret

Music: A. Meller
Lyrics: Y. Gamzu

Moderately

Em Am
A - hu - va - ti al mig - da - la - yich ha - g'vo - him pru - sa a -

C7-5 B7 Em G
de - ret ha - shki - ya s'mu - kat shu - la - yim ka - she ka - she she - lo li - yot bach n' - vi -

Am B F♯7 B
im o l' - fa - chot m' - sho - r' - rim Y' - ru - sha - la - yim ach bén cho -

Em Am C7-5 B7
za - yich she - nib - u bach no - a - shot et ha - mal - chut v' - et ha - dam v' - et ha -

Em G Am
che - rev a - ni ro - tse li - yot ha - ye - led ha - ri - shon she - yit - o -

B F♯7 B
rér bi - ru - sha - la - yim ha - a - che - ret Y' - ru - sha -

C (Am7) D7 Gmaj7 C 1. F♯m7-5
la - yim Y' - ru - sha - la - yim Y' - ru - sha - la - yim shel sha -

Em 2. F♯m7-5 Em
lom Y' - ru - sha - la - yim shel sha - lom

©by the authors

A-hu-va-ti al mig-da-la-yich ha-g'vo-him
P'-ru-sa a-de-ret ha-sh' ki-a s'-mu-kat shu-la-yim
Ka-she, ka-she she-lo li-yot bach n'-vi-im
O l'-fa-chot m'-sho-r'-rim Y'-ru-sha-la-yim

Ach bén cho-za-yich she-niv-u bach no-a-shot
Et ha-mal-chut v'-et ha-dam v'-et ha-che-rev
A-ni ro-tse li-yot ha-ye-led ha-ri-shon
She-yit-o-rér bi-ru-sha-la-yim ha-a-che-ret

Refrain
Y'-ru-sha-la-yim shel sha-lom

A-hu-va-ti mul bét ha-sé-fer l'-shot-rim
U-mul o-ta giv-at tach-mo-shet dam va-e-tsev
Et kol pits-é ha-cha-fi-rot k'-mo bit-fa-rim
Cho-vésh ha-z'man b'-tach-bo-shot k'-ri-rot shel é-sev
Refrain

אֲהוּבָתִי עַל מִגְדָּלַיִךְ הַגְּבוֹהִים
פְּרוּשָׂה אַדֶּרֶת הַשְּׁקִיעָה סְמוּקַת שׁוּלַיִם
קָשֶׁה, קָשֶׁה שֶׁלֹּא לִהְיוֹת בָּךְ נְבִיאִים
אוֹ לְפָחוֹת מְשׁוֹרְרִים יְרוּשָׁלַיִם

אַךְ בֵּין חוֹזַיִךְ שֶׁנִּבְּאוּ בָּךְ נוֹאָשׁוֹת
אֶת הַמַּלְכוּת וְאֶת הַדָּם וְאֶת הַחֶרֶב
אֲנִי רוֹצֶה לִהְיוֹת הַיֶּלֶד הָרִאשׁוֹן
שֶׁיִּתְעוֹרֵר בִּירוּשָׁלַיִם הָאַחֶרֶת

פזמון
יְרוּשָׁלַיִם שֶׁל שָׁלוֹם

אֲהוּבָתִי מוּל בֵּית הַסֵּפֶר לְשׁוֹטְרִים
וּמוּל אוֹתָהּ גִּבְעַת תַּחְמֹשֶׁת דָּם וָעֶצֶב
אֶת כָּל פִּצְעֵי הַחֲפִירוֹת כְּמוֹ בְּתַפְרִים
חוֹבֵשׁ הַזְּמַן בְּתַחְבּוֹשׁוֹת קְרִירוֹת שֶׁל עֵשֶׂב
פזמון

My beloved, the red mantle of dusk spreads upon your high towers. It is difficult, truly difficult, not to be a prophet, or at the very least, a poet within you Jerusalem.

Y'rushalayim Sheli

Music: N. Hirsh
Lyrics: D. Almagor

Moderately

Cm
A - mar ha - ro - chél mi - maz - ke - ret Mo - she Y' - ru - sha - la - yim she -

Cm Gm Cm Gm Cm
li______ hi Mach - 'ne Y' - hu - da b' - e - rev cha - gimj v' -

Gm Am7 - 5 D7 Gm B♭7 E♭
chu - mus shel Rach - mo v' - ré - ach da - gim v' - chu - mus shel Rach - mo v' -

B♭7 E♭ B♭7 E♭ Fm G
ré - ach da - gim Sha - bat shel po - pi - tas ki - l' - lot ne - ha - gim kvi -

Cm Am7 - 5 D7 G Fm6 G7
sa al ha - kvish u - mik - la - chat mi - dli Y' - ru - sha - la - yim she -

Cm
li______ Y' - ru - sha - la - yim Y' - ru - sha - la - yim

Cm
Y' - ru - sha - la - yim she - li______ Y' - ru - sha - la - yim she - li______

©by the authors

A-mar ha-ro-chél mi-maz-ke-ret Mo-she
Y'-ru-sha-la-yim she-li
Hi ma-cha-né Y'-hu-da b'-e-rev cha-gim
V'-chu-mus shel rach-mo v'-ré-ach da-gim
Sha-bat shel po-pi-tat kil-l'-lot ne-ha-gim
K'-vi-sa al hak-vish u-mik-la-chat mid-li
Refrain
Y'-ru-sha-la-yim, Y'-ru-sha-la-yim
Y'-ru-sha-la-yim she-li

אָמַר הָרוֹכֵל מִמַּזְכֶּרֶת מֹשֶׁה
יְרוּשָׁלַיִם שֶׁלִּי
הִיא מַחֲנֵה יְהוּדָה בְּעֶרֶב חַגִּים
וְחוּמוּס שֶׁל רַחְמוֹ וְרֵיחַ דָּגִים
שַׁבָּת שֶׁל פּוֹפִּיטַת קְלָלוֹת נֶהָגִים
כְּבִיסָה עַל הַכְּבִישׁ וּמִקְלַחַת מִדְּלִי
פזמון
יְרוּשָׁלַיִם, יְרוּשָׁלַיִם
יְרוּשָׁלַיִם שֶׁלִּי

A-mar ha-san-dlar mish-chu-nat ka-ta-mon
Y'-ru-sha-la-yim she-li
Hi she-va sha-nim shel g'-sha-mim ba-bil-kon
Shi-kun b'-li cha-nut o-to-bus b'li chesh-bon
Sha-bat ha-tsa-ga ri-sho-na b'-or-yon
Gam ka-ta-mon gim-el hi bish-vi-li Refrain

אָמַר הַסַּנְדְּלָר מִשְּׁכוּנַת קָטָמוֹן
יְרוּשָׁלַיִם שֶׁלִּי
הִיא שֶׁבַע שָׁנִים שֶׁל גְּשָׁמִים בַּבִּלְקוֹן
שִׁכּוּן בְּלִי חֲנוּת אוֹטוֹבּוּס בְּלִי חֶשְׁבּוֹן
שַׁבָּת הַצָּגָה רִאשׁוֹנָה בְּאוֹרְיוֹן
גַּם קָטָמוֹן ג׳ הִיא בִּשְׁבִילִי *פזמון*

A-mar ha-ba-lan mi-mé-a sh'-a-rim
Y'-ru-sha-la-yim she-li
Hi sh-trai-mel sha-chor u-sfa-rim a-fo-rim
U-"bat Yis-ra-él lo té-léch bik-tsa-rim"
Hi la-chash t'-fi-la l'-ya-mim a-ché-rim
Lo kan ki l'-ma-la ko-re-tset hi li Refrain

אָמַר הַבַּלָּן מִמֵּאָה שְׁעָרִים
יְרוּשָׁלַיִם שֶׁלִּי
הִיא שְׁטְרַיְמֶל שָׁחוֹר וּסְפָרִים אֲפֹרִים
וּ״בַּת יִשְׂרָאֵל לֹא תֵּלֵךְ בִּקְצָרִים״
הִיא לַחַשׁ תְּפִילָה לְיָמִים אֲחֵרִים
לֹא כָּאן כִּי לְמַעְלָה קוֹרֶצֶת הִיא לִי *פזמון*

A-mar ha-tsa-ir sham l'-yad sha-ar sh'-chem
Y'-ru-sha-la-yim she-li
Hi tslav al cha-nut v'-shot-rim ba-cha-tsot
A-chot she-hil-shi-na u-vor im p'-tsa-tsot
Mi-tsad ats-ma-ut v'-ya-da-yim k'-fu-tsot
"Yes sir! What, kebab or shishlik?" Refrain

אָמַר הַצָּעִיר שָׁם לְיַד שַׁעַר שְׁכֶם
יְרוּשָׁלַיִם שֶׁלִּי
הִיא צְלָב עַל חֲנוּת וְשׁוֹטְרִים בַּחֲצוֹת
אָחוֹת שֶׁהִלְשִׁינָה וּבוֹר עִם פְּצָצוֹת
מִצַּד עַצְמָאוּת וְיָדַיִם קְפוּצוֹת
״יֶס סֶר! ווֹט, קַבָּאב, אוֹר שִׁישְׁלִיק? *פזמון*

Amar ha-cha-yal mé-ash-dot Ya-a-kov
Y'-ru-sha-la-yim she-li
Ha-yi-ti ba pa-am ba-bo-ker shel sh'-chol
Sim-ta v'-tsa-laf bats-ri-ach mis-mol
Mé-az lo cha-zar-ti pa-shut lo ya-chol
Av-nér v'-ga-di— hém bish-vi-li

אָמַר הַחַיָּל מֵאַשְׁדּוֹת יַעֲקֹב
יְרוּשָׁלַיִם שֶׁלִּי
הָיִיתִי בָּהּ פַּעַם בַּבֹּקֶר שֶׁל שְׁכוֹל
סִמְטָה וְצַלָּף בִּצְרִיחַ מִשְּׂמֹאל
מֵאָז לֹא חָזַרְתִּי פָּשׁוּט לֹא יָכוֹל
אַבְנֵר וְגָדִי - הֵם בִּשְׁבִילִי *פזמון*

A peddler, a shoemaker, a bath attendant, a young man near the Damascus Gate and a soldier each describes Jerusalem from his own vantage point.

Avinu Malkénu

Music: Based on a Hassidic melody

Joyously

Dm | Bb | Dm C7 F

A - vi - nu mal - ké - nu sho - chén bam - ro - mim ya - vo ha - ma -

F Dm Gm Dm D7 Gm

shi - ach b' - shar ha - ra - cha - mim vi - la - dim nir - im m' - sa - cha - kim

C7 F Dm Gm Dm C

bir - cho - vot Tsi - yon ha - tso - cha - kim y' - hi sha - lom b' - ir - cha v' - shal - va b' -

A7 Dm Gm A7 Dm Dm

o - hal - cha mé - a - ta v' - ad o - lam___ la la la la la la la la

C Dm A7 Dm C7(A7) 1. F 2. Dm

la la la la la la la la la la la la la la la la la la la la___

A-vi-nu mal-ké-nu sho-chén bam-ro-mim
Ya-vo ha-ma-shi-ach b'-sha-ar ha-ra-cha-mim
Vi-la-dim nir-im m'-sa-cha-kim
Bir-cho-vot Tsi-yon ha-tso-cha-kim
Y'-hi sha-lom b'-ir-cha v'-shal-va b'-o-hal-cha
Mé-a-ta v'-ad o-lam

אָבִינוּ מַלְכֵּנוּ שׁוֹכֵן בַּמְּרוֹמִים
יָבֹא הַמָּשִׁיחַ בְּשַׁעַר הָרַחֲמִים
וִילָדִים נִרְאִים מְשַׂחֲקִים
בִּרְחוֹבוֹת צִיּוֹן הַצּוֹחֲקִים
יְהִי שָׁלוֹם בְּעִירְךָ וְשַׁלְוָה בְּאָהָלְךָ
מֵעַתָּה וְעַד עוֹלָם

Our merciful Father who dwells in heaven, grant us peace. Let the laughter of playing children be heard in the streets of Zion. Let there be peace in Your city and tranquillity within Your home now and forever.

En Kirushalayim

Music: C. Parchi
Lyrics: A. Broides

Allegro

C C7 F G7 C
En ki - ru - sha - la - yim kir - yat cho - zim v' - él

C C/E F Dm Gsus G7 C
a - chat Y' - ru - sha - la - yim lév E - rets Yis - ra - él

C7 C/E F Dm G C
a - chat Y' - ru - sha - la - yim lév E - rets Yis - ra - él

F C/ E Dm7 G C7
la la la la la la la la la la la la la la la

F C/ E G7 C
la la la la la la la la la la

© by the author

Én ki-ru-sha-la-yim
Kir-yat cho-zim v'-él
A-chat Y'-ru-sha-la-yim
Lév e-retsYis-ra-él

אֵין כִּירוּשָׁלַיִם
קִרְיַת חוֹזִים וְאֵל
אַחַת יְרוּשָׁלַיִם
לֵב אֶרֶץ יִשְׂרָאֵל

There is no place like Jerusaelm, city of seers and God.
There is only one Jerusalem, heart of the land of Israel.

En Kirushyalayim II

Music: E. Ben Hayim
Lyrics: A. Broides

© by the authors

Én ki-ru-sha-la-yim kir-yat cho-zim va-él
A-chat Y'-ru-sha-la-yim tsur E-rets Yis-ra-él
Én ki-ru-sha-la-yim tif-e-ret bam am v'-am
A-chat Y'-ru-sha-la-yim li-bé-nu la yif-am
Én ki-ru-sha-la-yim ir ko-desh l'-chu-lam
A-chat Y'-ru-sha-la-yim la-nu ba-o-lam

אֵין כִּירוּשָׁלַיִם קִרְיַת חוֹזִים וָאֵל
אַחַת יְרוּשָׁלַיִם צוּר אֶרֶץ יִשְׂרָאֵל
אֵין כִּירוּשָׁלַיִם תִּפְאֶרֶת עַם וָעָם
אַחַת יְרוּשָׁלַיִם לִבֵּנוּ לָהּ יִפְעַם
אֵין כִּירוּשָׁלַיִם עִיר קֹדֶשׁ לְכֻלָּם
אַחַת יְרוּשָׁלַיִם לָנוּ בָּעוֹלָם

There is no city like Jerusalem, holy city to all. There is one Jerusalem to all of us in the world.

Shémot Harbé Lirushalayim

Music: N. Hirsh
Lyrics: D. Almagor

Moderately

Dm Dm/C Gm/B♭ F/C B♭6 Gm7
Shé - mot har - bé li - ru - sha - la - yim v' - chol shém na -

A7 Dm Dm Dm/C Gm/B♭ F/C B♭6 Gm7
e mé - cha - vé - ro shé - mot har - bé li - ru - sha - la - yim v' - chol shém na -

A7 Dm C/E F
e mi - cha - vé - ro kir - yat Me - lech Ram kir - ya ne - e - ma - na m' -

Dm C7 F A7 Dm B♭
sos kol ha - a - rets ir ba Da - vid cha - na kir - yat Me - lech Ram kir -

C7 F Gm Gm7 A7 Dm
ya ne - e - ma - na m' - sos kol ha - a - rets ir ba Da - vid cha - na

©by the authors

Shé-mot har-bé li-ru-sha-la-yim	שְׁמוֹת הַרְבֵּה לִירוּשָׁלַיִם
V'-chol shém na-e mé-cha-vé-ro	וְכָל שֵׁם נָאֶה מֵחֲבֵרוֹ
Kir-yat me-lech ram	קִרְיַת מֶלֶךְ רָם
Kir-ya ne-e-ma-na	קִרְיָה נֶאֱמָנָה
M'-sos kol ha-a-rets	מְשׂוֹשׂ כָּל הָאָרֶץ
Ir ba Da-vid cha-na	עִיר בָּהּ דָּוִד חָנָה
Shé-mot har-bé li-ru-sha-la-yim	שְׁמוֹת הַרְבֵּה לִירוּשָׁלַיִם
V'-chol shém ya-fe mé-cha-vé-ro	וְכָל שֵׁם יָפֶה מֵחֲבֵרוֹ
Y'-fé nof ke-ter be-ha-rim	יְפֵה נוֹף כֶּתֶר בֶּהָרִים
A-ri-él ir shel za-hav	אֲרִיאֵל עִיר שֶׁל זָהָב
V'-im na-vo, na-vo lim-not ha-yom	וְאִם נָבוֹא, נָבוֹא לִמְנוֹת הַיּוֹם
Et kol sh'-mo-te-ha shel Y'-ru-sha-la-yim	אֶת כָּל שְׁמוֹתֶיהָ שֶׁל יְרוּשָׁלַיִם
Yich-le ha-n'-yar v'-ti-vash ha-d'-yo	יִכְלֶה הַנְּיָר וְתִיבַשׁ הַדְּיוֹ
V'-ti-ga kol yad v'-has lo yich-lu	וְתִיגַע כָּל יָד וְהַס לֹא יִכְלוּ
Na-e mi-kol ha-shé-mot	נָאֶה מִכֹּל, מִכֹּל הַשֵּׁמוֹת
Na-e mi-kol- ha-shém Y'-ru-sha-la-yim	נָאֶה מִכֹּל- הַשֵּׁם יְרוּשָׁלַיִם

Jerusalem has many names, each one more beautiful than the other.

L'chol Echad Y'rushalayim

Music: M. Amarilio
Lyrics: N. Yonatan

Moderately

A D A
L' - chol e - chad yésh ir u - shma Y' - ru - sha - la - yim_____ she -

E7 C7
hu o - lém_____ o - lém la cha - lo - mot_____ ad she - ta - a -

Fm B♭m
le ba - har pri - chat ha - la - yil_____ v' - ta - ir lo ba - a - rov yo -

E E7 C7 Fm
mo_____ ad she - ta - a - le ba - har pri - chat ha - la - yil_____

Bm E7
_____ v' - ta - ir lo ba - a - rov yo - mo_____ mé -

A E7 A
a - fa - réch_____ Y' - ru - sha - la - yim_____ ya - i - ru lo_____

E7 A E7 A
_____ pir - ché ha - la - yil . . . oo . . . .

D A E7 A
oo . . . .

©by the authors

L'-chol e-chad yésh ir u-shma Y'-ru-sha-la-yim
She-hu o-lém, o-lém la cha-lo-mot
Ad she-ta-a-le ba-har pri-chat ha-la-yil
V'-ta-ir lo ba-a-rov yo-mo
Mé-a-fa-réch Y'-ru-sha-la-yim
Ya-i-ru lo pir-ché ha-la-yil

לְכָל אֶחָד יֵשׁ עִיר וּשְׁמָהּ יְרוּשָׁלַיִם
שֶׁהוּא אוֹלֵם, אוֹלֵם לָהּ חֲלוֹמוֹת
עַד שֶׁתַּעֲלֶה בָּהָר פְּרִיחַת הַלַּיִל
וְתָאִיר לוֹ בַּעֲרוֹב יוֹמוֹ
מֵעֲפָרֵךְ יְרוּשָׁלַיִם
יָאִירוּ לוֹ פִּרְחֵי הַלַּיִל

L'-chol e-chad yesh-no ma-kom bi-ru-sha-la-yim
She-hu ko-ré, ko-ré lo a-ha-va
K'-she-ya-vo ba-sof ya-chéf v'-kar é-la-yich
Yim-t'-ku ha-or v'-ha-a-vak
Mé-a-fa-réch Y'-ru-sha-la-yim
Ya-i-ru lo pir-ché ha-la-yil

לְכָל אֶחָד יֶשְׁנוֹ מָקוֹם בִּירוּשָׁלַיִם
שֶׁהוּא קוֹרֵא, קוֹרֵא לוֹ אַהֲבָה
כְּשֶׁיָּבוֹא בַּסּוֹף יָחֵף וְקַר אֵלַיִךְ
יִמְתְּקוּ הָאוֹר וְהָאָבָק
מֵעֲפָרֵךְ יְרוּשָׁלַיִם
יָאִירוּ לוֹ פִּרְחֵי הַלַּיִל

Yesh-na ats-vut u-sh'-ma do-me li-ru-sha-la-yim
U-vin-gi-nat ts-li-lé pa-a-mo-nim
Shir a-cha-ron yé-réd mi-go-va mig-da-la-yich
L'-na-gén et sh'mo ba-a-va-nim
Mé-a-fa-réch Y'-ru-sha-la-yim
Ya-i-ru lo pir-ché ha-la-yil

יֶשְׁנָהּ עַצְבוּת וּשְׁמָהּ דּוֹמֶה לִירוּשָׁלַיִם
וּבִנְגִינַת צְלִילֵי פַּעֲמוֹנִים
שִׁיר אַחֲרוֹן יֵרֵד מִגֹּבַהּ מִגְדָּלַיִךְ
לְנַגֵּן אֶת שְׁמוֹ בָּאֲבָנִים
מֵעֲפָרֵךְ יְרוּשָׁלַיִם
יָאִירוּ לוֹ פִּרְחֵי הַלַּיִל

For each individual there is a city and its name is Jerusalem. There dreams are woven until the night flowers open upon the mountain and illuminate the evening. From your dust Jerusalem the night flowers will shine.

Al Kapav Yavi

Music: Y. Rosenblum
Lyrics: Y. Tahar-Lev

Andante

Am Dm G
Bir - cho - vé - nu ha - tsar gar na - gar e - chad mu - zar hu yo -

C E7 Am Dm E Am
shév bits - ri - fo v' - lo o - se da - var ish é - no ba lik - not v' - én

Dm7 G7 E7 Am Dm E7
ish m' - va - kér u - sh'na - ta - yim she - hu k'var é - no m' - na -

Am Dm7 Em
gér___ v' - hu cha - lom e - chad no - sé od bil - va - vo___ liv - not ki -

Dm7 G7 C Dm E7 Am
sé l' - é - li - ya - hu she - ya - vo al ka - pav o - to ya - vi

Gm7 E E7 Am
l' - é - li - ya - hu ha - na - vi v' - hu yo - shév u - m' - cha -

Dm G7 C Am
ke lo k'var sha - nim cho - lém hu she - yiz - ke lo al so -

©by the authors

Bir-cho-vé-nu ha-tsar gar na-gar e-chad mu-zar
Hu yo-shév bits-ri-fo v'-lo o-se da-var
Ish é-no ba lik-not v'-én ish m'-va-kér
Ush-na-ta-yim she-hu k'-var é-no m'-na-gér
V'-hu cha-lom e-chad no-sé od bil-va-vo
Liv-not ki-sé l'-é-li-ya-hu she-ya-vo
Al ka-pav o-to-ya-vi
L'-é-li-ya-hu ha-na-vi
Refrain
V'-hu yo-shév u-m'-cha-ke lo
K'-var sha-nim cho-lém hu she-yiz-ke lo
Al so-do sho-mér u-m'-cha-ke lo
Ma-tai k'-var ya-gi-a ha-yom

Bir-cho-vé-nu ha-tsar gar san-dlar e-chad mu-zar
Hu yo-shév bits-ri-fo v'-lo o-se da-var
Ma-da-fav ha-ré-kim m'-chu-sim ba-a-vak
K'-var shna-ta-yim mu-nach ha-mar-tsé-a ba-sak
V'-hu cho-lém ki na-a-la-yim hu to-fér
Ban al ha-rim yin-vu rag-lé ha-m'-va-ser
Al ka-pav o-tan ya-vi
L'-é-li-ya-hu ha-na-vi Refrain

בִּרְחוֹבֵנוּ הַצָּר גָּר נַגָּר אֶחָד מוּזָר
הוּא יוֹשֵׁב בִּצְרִיפוֹ וְלֹא עוֹשֶׂה דָּבָר
אִישׁ אֵינוֹ בָּא לִקְנוֹת וְאֵין אִישׁ מְבַקֵּר
וּשְׁנָתַיִם שֶׁהוּא כְּבָר אֵינוֹ מְנַגֵּר
וְהוּא חֲלוֹם אֶחָד נוֹשֵׂא עוֹד בִּלְבָבוֹ
לִבְנוֹת כִּסֵּא לְאֵלִיָּהוּ שֶׁיָּבוֹא
עַל כַּפָּיו אֹתוֹ יָבִיא
לְאֵלִיָּהוּ הַנָּבִיא
פזמון
וְהוּא יוֹשֵׁב וּמְחַכֶּה לוֹ
כְּבָר שָׁנִים חוֹלֵם הוּא שֶׁיִּזְכֶּה לוֹ
עַל סוֹדוֹ שׁוֹמֵר וּמְחַכֶּה לוֹ
מָתַי כְּבָר יַגִּיעַ הַיּוֹם

בִּרְחוֹבֵנוּ הַצָּר גָּר סַנְדְּלָר אֶחָד מוּזָר
הוּא יוֹשֵׁב בִּצְרִיפוֹ וְלֹא עוֹשֶׂה דָּבָר
מַדָּפָיו הָרֵיקִים מְכֻסִּים בָּאָבָק
כְּבָר שְׁנָתַיִם מוּנָח הַמַּרְצֵעַ בַּשָּׂק
וְהוּא חוֹלֵם כִּי נַעֲלַיִם הוּא תּוֹפֵר
בָּן עַל הָרִים יִנְווּ רַגְלֵי הַמְבַשֵּׂר
עַל כַּפָּיו אֹתָן יָבִיא
לְאֵלִיָּהוּ הַנָּבִיא *פזמון*

A carpenter and a shoemaker sit idle day after day dreaming and waiting for the coming of Elijah. The carpenter dreams that he will build him a special chair. The shoemaker will make a special pair of shoes which the prophet will wear when he announces good tidings for Israel.

Additional text see page 187

Bisharayich Y'rushalayim

Music: Y. Gamzu
Lyrics: Y. Braun

Moderately

Cm Fm6 Cm E♭
Om - dot rag - lé - nu bish - a - ra - yich Y' - ru - sha - la - yim___ v' - to - ta -

Fm G7 Cm Cm
ché - nu mar - i - mim lach shir miz - mor v' - rak dim - ot ha - ga - a -

Cm E♭ C7 Fm Cm B♭ E♭
va she - ba - é - na - yim___ not - fot du - mam al ha - ma - dim v' - he - cha - gor

G7 Cm Gm Cm B♭7 E♭
Tsi - yon ha - lo tish - a - li lish - lom ba - chu - ra - yich Tsi -

A♭ B♭ E♭ C7 Fm
yon ze ha - o - sher sho - ég b' - cha - zé - nu pir - i lam - na -

Cm Fm E♭ Cm
tsé - ach miz - mor lam - na - tsé - ach al mik - la al mik - la v' - ri - mon bish - a -

Gm Cm B♭ E♭ Fm7 G7 Cm
ra - yich b' - da - mé - nu cha - yi b' - da - mé - nu cha - yi

© by the authors

Om-dot rag-lé-nu bish-a-ra-yich Y'-ru-sha-la-yim
V'-to-ta-ché-nu mar-i-mim lach shir miz-mor
V'-rak dim-ot ha-ga-a-va she-ba-é-na-yim
Not-fot du-mam al ha-ma-dim v'-he-cha-gor
Refrain
Tsi-yon ha-lo tish-a-li lish-lom ba-chu-ra-yich
Tsi-yon ze ha-o-sher sho-ég b'-cha-zé-nu pir-i
Lam-na-tsé-ach miz-mor al mik-la v'-ri-mon bish-a-a-ra-yich
B'-da-mé-nu cha-yi, b'-da-mé-nu cha-yi

Mi-shéch Ja-rach ad Nebi Sa-mu-él la-yil la-yil
Ha-yu ru-chot ta-shach sha-rot lach b'-dar-chan
Im esh-ka-chéch...im esh-ka-chéch Y'-ru-sha-la-yim
Ach lo sha-chach-nu v'-ha-ré a-nach-nu kan Refrain

עוֹמְדוֹת הָיוּ רַגְלֵינוּ בִּשְׁעָרַיִךְ יְרוּשָׁלַיִם
וְתוֹתָחֵינוּ מַרְעִימִים לָךְ שִׁיר מִזְמוֹר
וְרַק דִּמְעוֹת הַגַּאֲוָה שֶׁבָּעֵינַיִם
נוֹטְפוֹת דוּמָם עַל הַמַּדִּים וְהֶחָגוֹר
פזמון
צִיּוֹן הֲלֹא תִשְׁאֲלִי לִשְׁלוֹם בַּחוּרַיִךְ
צִיּוֹן זֶה הָאֹשֶׁר שׁוֹאֵג בְּחָזֵנוּ פִּרְאִי
לַמְנַצֵּחַ מִזְמוֹר עַל מִקְלָע וְרִמּוֹן בִּשְׁעָרַיִךְ
בְּדָמֵנוּ חַיִי, בְּדָמֵנוּ חַיִי

מִשֵּׁיךְ גַּ׳רַאח עַד נֶבִּי סַמוּאֵל לַיִל לַיִל
הָיוּ רוּחוֹת תַּשַׁ״ח שָׁרוֹת לָךְ בְּדַרְכָּן:
אִם אֶשְׁכָּחֵךְ.....אִם אֶשְׁכָּחֵךְ יְרוּשָׁלַיִם
אַךְ לֹא שָׁכַחְנוּ-וְהֲרֵי אֲנַחְנוּ כַּאן *פזמון*

We stand at the gates of Jerusalem and our cannons roar your praise. We have not forgotten you Jerusalem.

Ani, Y'rushalayim

O. Bat Chaim

© by the author

Omrim-
She-én shni-ya li
Ha-rim sa-viv li
Yof-yi ma-lé hod
Om-rim-
She-ré-chi tsa-lul ka-ya-yin
Ku-lam bi cha-fé-tsim
Mit-pa-l'-lim l'-ma-an sh'-lo-mi
Om-rim-
She-ko-chi rav u-m'-sha-kér
She-mi she-ro-é-ni mit-ba-sem
Mi-ru-chi mit-a-le mit-ro-mém
Om-rim-
"Im esh-ka-chéch Y'-ru-sha-la-yim
Tish-kach y'-mi-ni
Tid-bak l'-sho-ni l'-chi-ki"
Om-rim ze al-fé sha-nim
Om-rim-
She-o-ha-vai mé-tim l'-ma-a-ni
Kol e-chad mi-me-ni
Cha-ti-cha ro-tse la-ka-chat
Va-a-ni sach ha-kol
N'-ku-da a-chat k'-ta-na
Mé-i-ra b'-or ha-sh'-chi-na
A-le-ha so-vév
Tsi-ro shel o-lam
A-ni, Y'-ru-sha-la-yim

They say-
There is no other like me
Hills surround me
My beauty is splendid
They say-
My scent is clear as wine
All yearn for me
Praying for my peace
They say-
My strength is great and inspiring
For he who sees me is bathed in perfume
From my spirit he rises and ascends
The say-
"If I forget thee O Jerusalem
Let my right hand forget its cunning
Let my tongue cleave to the roof of my mouth"
For thousands of years
They say-
That those who love me
Die for me
All wish to have a part of me
And I am merely a tiny spot
Bright with the light of *Sh'china*
Which spins the universe round
I, Jerusalem

אוֹמְרִים-
שֶׁאֵין שְׁנִיָּה לִי
הָרִים סָבִיב לִי
יוֹפְיִי מָלֵא הוֹד
אוֹמְרִים-
שֶׁרֵיחִי צָלוּל כַּיַּיִן
כֻּלָּם בִּי חֲפֵצִים
מִתְפַּלְּלִים לְמַעַן שְׁלוֹמִי
אוֹמְרִים-
שֶׁכֹּחִי רַב וּמְשַׁקֵּר
שֶׁמִּי שֶׁרוֹאֵנִי מִתְבַּשֵּׂם
מֵרוּחִי מִתְעַלֶּה מִתְרוֹמֵם
אוֹמְרִים-
"אִם אֶשְׁכָּחֵךְ יְרוּשָׁלַיִם
תִּשְׁכַּח יְמִינִי
תִּדְבַּק לְשׁוֹנִי לְחִכִּי"
זֶה אַלְפֵי שָׁנִים
אוֹמְרִים-
שֶׁאֹהֲבַי מֵתִים לְמַעֲנִי
כָּל אֶחָד מִמֶּנִּי
חֲתִיכָה רוֹצֶה לָקַחַת
וַאֲנִי סַךְ הַכֹּל
נְקוּדָה אַחַת קְטַנָּה
מְאִירָה בְּאוֹר הַשְּׁכִינָה
עָלֶיהָ סוֹבֵב
צִירוֹ שֶׁל עוֹלָם
אֲנִי, יְרוּשָׁלַיִם

Hal'lu Lirushalayim

C. Parchi

© by the author

Ha-l'-lu li-ru-sha-la-yim
Ha-l'-lu na l'-tsi-yon
Ku-mu v'-na-a-le Tsi-yon

הַלְלוּ לִירוּשָׁלַיִם
הַלְלוּ נָא לְצִיּוֹן
קוּמוּ וְנַעֲלֶה צִיּוֹן

Praised be Jerusalem! Praised be Zion!
Arise and let us go up to Zion.

The Colors of Jerusalem

F. Avni

Moderately

C Dm Em Dm C Dm C

Loo loo loo lo___

C Dm C Dm C Dm C

loo loo loo loo___

Dm Em Dm6 Dm C Dm

We're all chil - dren of Cre - a -

C Dm C Dm C C Dm

tion___ sons and daugh - ters of wo - man and man though we've wan - dered far from

C Dm C Dm C Am F

E - den we must do the best___ we can___ to pre - serve the won - ders of

G F Dm C Am

na - ture and the pro - mis - es___ of old___ and the co - ve - nant___ of our

F C Dm G7 C F C F

an - ces - tors in Da - vid's ci - ty of gold___ and the

© by the author

We're all children of Creation, sons and daughters of woman and man
Though we've wandered far from Eden we must do the best we can
To preserve the wonders of nature and the promises of old
And the covenant of our ancestors in David's city of Gold
And the colors of Jerusalem are wondrous to behold
Each day at sunrise and sunset all its hills are filled with gold
And everyone can be a poet or painter adding their own special hue
To two thousand years of hopes and dreams that color its mighty view
Ha-ir Y'-ru-sha-la-yim hi m'-lé-a ha-mon tsva-im
Shel ke-shet brit a-vo-té-nu tik-vot shel al-fé sha-nim
V'-chol e-chad mo-sif tiv o-ga-van lo rak m'-sho-r'-rim
La-ir b'ru-cha Ha-l'-lu-ya Y'-ru-sha-la-yim

Erets Yisraél Yafa

Music: Y. Paikov
Lyrics: D. Barak

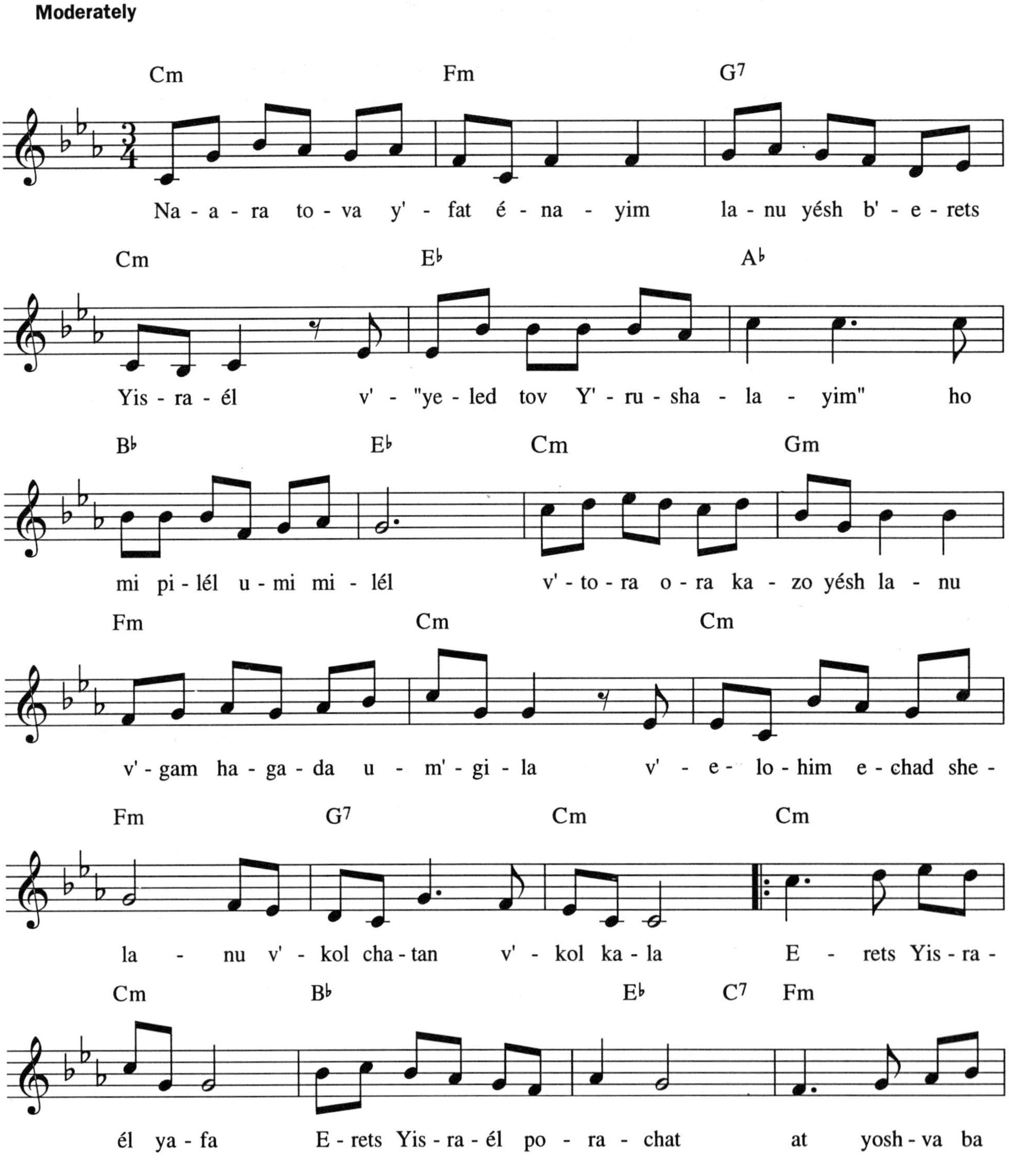

Cm Fm G7
Na - a - ra to - va y' - fat é - na - yim la - nu yésh b' - e - rets

Cm E♭ A♭
Yis - ra - él v' - "ye - led tov Y' - ru - sha - la - yim" ho

B♭ E♭ Cm Gm
mi pi - lél u - mi mi - lél v' - to - ra o - ra ka - zo yésh la - nu

Fm Cm Cm
v' - gam ha - ga - da u - m' - gi - la v' - e - lo - him e - chad she -

Fm G7 Cm Cm
la - nu v' - kol cha - tan v' - kol ka - la E - rets Yis - ra -

Cm B♭ E♭ C7 Fm
él ya - fa E - rets Yis - ra - él po - ra - chat at yosh - va ba

Cm G7 Cm

v' - tso - fa at tso - fa ba v' - zo - ra - chat

©by the authors

Na-a-ra to-va y'-fat é-na-yim	נַעֲרָה טוֹבָה יְפַת עֵינַיִם
La-nu yésh b'-e-rets Yis-ra-él	לָנוּ יֵשׁ בְּאֶרֶץ יִשְׂרָאֵל
V'-ye-led tov Y'-ru-sha-la-yim	ו״יֶלֶד טוֹב יְרוּשָׁלַיִם״
Ho mi pi-lél u-mi mi-lél	הוֹ מִי פִּלֵּל וּמִי מִלֵּל
V'-to-ra o-ra ka-zo yésh la-nu	וְתוֹרָה אוֹרָה כָּזוֹ יֵשׁ לָנוּ
V'-gam ha-ga-da u-m'-gi-la	וְגַם הַגָּדָה וּמְגִלָּה
V'e-lo-him e-chad she-la-nu	וֵאלֹהִים אֶחָד שֶׁלָּנוּ
V'-kol cha-tan v'-kol ka-la	וְקוֹל חָתָן וְקוֹל כַּלָּה
Refrain	פזמון
E-rets Yisrael ya-fa	אֶרֶץ יִשְׂרָאֵל יָפָה
E-rets Yis-ra-él po-ra-chat	אֶרֶץ יִשְׂרָאֵל פּוֹרַחַת
At yosh-va ba v'-tso-fa	אַתְּ יוֹשְׁבָה בָּהּ וְצוֹפָה
At tso-fa ba v'-zo-ra-chat	אַתְּ צוֹפָה בָּהּ וְזוֹרַחַת

We have a fair-eyed girl in the Land of Israel. We have the light of Torah and Haggadah and Megillah. We have one God and the voice of bridegroom and bride. Beautiful, flowering Land of Israel, you dwell there and look forth, you look forth and shine.

Kinor David

Music & Lyrics: A. Medina

Allegro moderato

Dm G C
Lif - né sha - nim ra - bot sham - u b' - e - retz Yis - ra -

Dm E7 Am
él ko - lot ni - gun shi - ra u - miz - mo - rim bi -

Dm C Dm C
ts'lil ko - m' - yu - chad u - vin - i - ma___ to - va k' -

Dm C Dm
shir tsi - por za - mir bén he - a - lim bi - ts'lil ko m' - yu -

Em Dm G C
chad u - vin - i - ma___ to - va k' - shir tsi - por za -

Em Am Am Am
mir bén he - a - lim_______ ze ki - nor Da - vid b' - yad___ Da - vid ha - me - lech ha -

© by the author

Lif-né sha-nim ra-bot sham-u b'-e-rets Yis-ra-él
Ko-lot ni-gun shi-ra u-miz-mo-rim
Bits-lil ko-m'-yu-chad u-vin-i-ma to-va
K'-shir tsi-por za-mir bén he-a-lim

Refrain
Ze ki-nor Da-vid b'-yad Da-vid ha-me-lech
Ha-po-rét al mé-ta-rav
K'-tov li-bo v'-ya-yin l'-ét e-rev
M'-la-ve hu et shi-rav

Lif-né sha-nim ra-bot b'-sha-a-ré Y'-ru-sha-la-yim
Nits-va nif-e-met ba-cha-lon mi-chal
Hi-bi-ta ba-mish-ol u-v'-é-ne-ha or
Ro-kéd Da-vid u-v'-ya-do ki-nor Refrain

לִפְנֵי שָׁנִים רַבּוֹת שָׁמְעוּ בְּאֶרֶץ יִשְׂרָאֵל
קוֹלוֹת נִגּוּן שִׁירָה וּמִזְמוֹרִים
בְּצְלִיל כֹּה מְיוּחָד וּבִנְעִימָה טוֹבָה
כְּשִׁיר צִפּוֹר זָמִיר בֵּין הֶעָלִים

פזמון
זֶה כִּנּוֹר דָּוִד בְּיַד דָּוִד הַמֶּלֶךְ
הַפּוֹרֵט עַל מֵיתָרָיו
כְּטוֹב לִבּוֹ בְּיַיִן לְעֵת עֶרֶב
מְלַוֶּה הוּא אֶת שִׁירָיו

לִפְנֵי שָׁנִים רַבּוֹת בְּשַׁעֲרֵי יְרוּשָׁלַיִם
נִצְּבָה נִפְעֶמֶת בַּחַלּוֹן מִיכַל
הִבִּיטָה בַּמִּשְׁעוֹל וּבְעֵינֶיהָ אוֹר
רוֹקֵד דָּוִד וּבְיָדוֹ כִּנּוֹר

Many years ago a beautiful song was heard in the land of Israel. This is the harp of David which accompanied his songs when his heart was gladdened with wine.

Or Virushalayim

Y. Sarig

Dm Gm Dm
Ha - she - ket shuv tso - né - ach kan bish - mé ha - e - rev___ k' - d' - i -

Gm7 C7 F C7 Gm Gdim
at da - ya mé - al ha - t' - ho - mot_____ v' - she - mesh a - du - ma no - she - ket la - hat

G♯dim A7 B♭m7 Gm A Dm C
che - rev___ et ha - p'sa - got ha - mig - da - lim v' - ha - cho - mot______ ra - i - ta

F E7 A Dm6 C7
ir_______ o - te - fet or_______ v' - hi o - la bish - lal tsiv - é___ ha -

F D7 Gm A7 B♭ Gm6
ke - shet___ v' - hi - no - ge - net bi k' - né - vel___ he - a - sor______ ra - i - ti

G♯dim E7 Asus A7 F E7
ir________ o - te - fet or_________ ra - i - ti ir_________ o - te - fet

A A7 Dm C F D7
or______ v' - hi o - la bish - lal tsiv - é ha - ke - shet____ v' - hi - no -

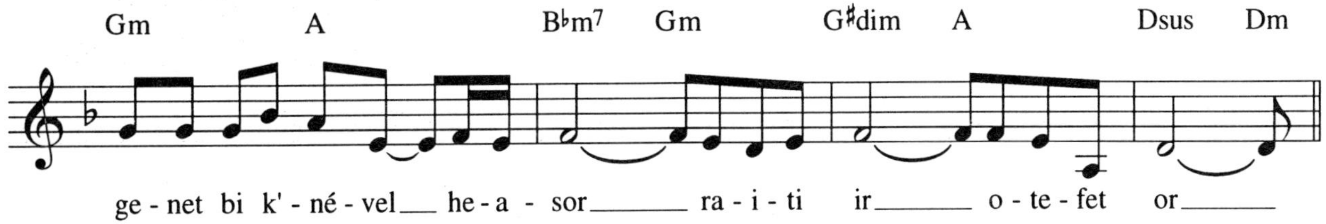

© by the author

Ha-she-ket shuv tso-né-ach kan bish-mé ha-e-rev
K'-d'-i-yat da-ya mé-al ha-t'-ho-mot
V'-she-mesh a-du-ma no-she-ket la-hat che-rev
Et haf-sa-got ha-mig-da-lim v'-ha-cho-mot
Refrain
Ra-i-ti ir o-te-fet or
V'-hi o-la bish-lal tsiv-é ha-ke-shet
V'-hi no-ge-net bi ch'-né-vel he-a-sor
Ra-i-ti ir o-te-fet or

Hi-né zo-chél ha-tsél mi-bén giv-ot ha-o-ren
Ka-rév ba-sé-ter k'-o-hév el hash-chu-not
U-mul pa-nav k'-ri-tsot ri-bo é-né ha-or hén
L'-fe-ta nif-k'-chu é-lai k'-nif-a-mot Refrain

B'-du-mi- yat esh-mo-ra a-cha-ro-na no-she-met
U-vik-ti-fat sh'-cha-kim r'-sis a-cha-ron ma-cha-vir
Ach sha-char k'-var ki-pat za-hav she-la o-de-met
L'-ma-ga-o ha-cham ha-rach nshel or tsa-ir Refrain

הַשֶּׁקֶט שׁוּב צוֹנֵחַ כָּאן בִּשְׁמֵי הָעֶרֶב
כְּדְאִיַּת דַּיָּה מֵעַל הַתְּהוֹמוֹת
וְשֶׁמֶשׁ אֲדֻמָּה נוֹשֶׁקֶת לַהַט חֶרֶב
אֶת הַפִּסְגוֹת הַמִּגְדָּלִים וְהַחוֹמוֹת
פזמון
רָאִיתִי עִיר עוֹטֶפֶת אוֹר
וְהִיא עוֹלָה בְּשַׁלַּל צִבְעֵי הַקֶּשֶׁת
וְהִיא נוֹגֶנֶת בִּי כְּנֵבֶל הֶעָשׂוֹר
רָאִיתִי עִיר עוֹטֶפֶת אוֹר

הִנֵּה זוֹחֵל הַצֵּל מִבֵּין גִּבְעוֹת הָאֹרֶן
קָרֵב בַּסֵּתֶר כְּאוֹהֵב אֶל הַשְּׁכוּנוֹת
וּמוּל פָּנָיו קְרִיצוֹת רִבּוֹא עֵינֵי הָאוֹר הֵן
לְפֶתַע נִפְקְחוּ אֵלַי כִּנְפְעָמוֹת *פזמון*

בְּדוּמִיַּת אַשְׁמוֹרָה אַחֲרוֹנָה נוֹשֶׁמֶת
וּבִקְטִיפַת שְׁחָקִים רְסִיס אַחֲרוֹן מַחֲוִיר
אַךְ שַׁחַר כְּבָר כִּפַּת זָהָב שֶׁלָּה אוֹדֶמֶת
לְמַגָּעוֹ הַחַם הָרַךְ שֶׁל אוֹר צָעִיר *פזמון*

Silence again descends in the evening sky like a kite gliding above the deep. The red sun kisses the blazing sword, the peaks, the towers, the walls. I saw a city wrapped in light, arising in rainbow colors. It plays on me like a ten stringed harp. I saw a city wrapped in light.

Tsiyon Tamati

M. Dulitzky

Moderately

Gm Dm A7 Dm Gm
Tsi - yon ta - ma - ti Tsi - yon chem - da - ti lach naf - shi mé -

Dm D7 Gm C F
ra - chok ho - mi - ya tish - kach y' - mi - ni im esh-

C6 F Dm C Dm Dm
ka - chéch ya - fa - ti ad te - a - tar bor kiv - ri a - lai pi - ha

B♭ Cm Gm
Tsi - yon ta - ma - ti Tsi - yon chem - da - ti lach naf - shi mé -

Cm D7 Gm D7 Gm C F
ra - chok ho - mi - ya tish - kach y' - mi - ni im esh-

C6 F Dm C Dm A7 Dm
ka - chéch ya - fa - ti ad te - a - tar bor kiv - ri a - lai pi - ha

©by the author

Tsi-yon ta-ma-ti Tsi-yon chem-da-ti
Lach naf-shi mé-ra-chok ho-mi-ya
Tish-kach y'-mi-ni im esh-ka-chéch ya-fa-ti
Ad te-a-tar bor kiv-ri a-lai pi-ha

Tid-bak ad mo-ti l'-chi-ki l'-sho-ni
Im lo ez-k'-ré-chi bat Tsi-yon ha-n'-sha-ma
Yi-vash l'-va-vi mé-cha-li mé-o-ni
Im ti-vash al on-yéch dim-a-ti ha-cha-ma

צִיוֹן תַּמָתִי צִיוֹן חֶמְדָתִי
לָךְ נַפְשִׁי מֵרָחוֹק הוֹמִיָה
תִּשְׁכַּח יְמִינִי אִם אֶשְׁכָּחֵךְ יָפָתִי
עַד תֶּאֱטַר בּוֹר קִבְרִי עָלַי פִּיהָ

תִּדְבַּק עַד מוֹתִי לְחִכִּי לְשׁוֹנִי
אִם לֹא אֶזְכְּרֵכִי בַּת צִיוֹן הַנְּשָׁמָה
יִיבַשׁ לְבָבִי מֵחֳלִי מְעוֹנִי
אִם תִּיבַשׁ עַל עֵנַיִךְ דִּמְעָתִי הַחַמָּה

My perfect Zion, my pleasant Zion, may my right hand forget its cunning if I forget you. I will not forget you Zion; I will not forget you my perfect one.

FROM THE BIBLE AND LITURGY

SCHOKEN BIBLE • SOUTHERN GERMANY C. 1300

Uva'u Ha'ovdim

Music: S. Carlebach
Lyrics: Isaiah 27:13

Joyously

Dm Gm Dm Gm Dm

U - va - u ha - ov - dim b' - e - rets a - shur v' - ha - ni - da - chim b' -

F Gm

e - rets mits - ra - yim v' - hish - ta - cha - vu la - shem b' - har ha - ko - desh

Gm 1. C F 2. C7 F

v' - hish - ta - cha vu la - shem b' - har ha - ko - desh b' - har ha - ko - desh bi -

D7 Gm C F

ru - sha - la - yim bi - ru - sha - la - yim bi -

D7 Gm Am A7 1. Dm 2. Dm

ru - sha - la - yim bi - ru - sha - la - yim bi - yim

© by the author

U-va-u ha-ov-dim b'-e-rets a-shur
V'-ha-ni-da-chim b'-e-rets mits-ra-yim
V'-hish-ta-cha-vu la-shem b'-har ha-ko-desh
Bi-ru-sha-la-yim

וּבָאוּ הָאֹבְדִים בְּאֶרֶץ אַשּׁוּר
וְהַנִּדָּחִים בְּאֶרֶץ מִצְרָיִם
וְהִשְׁתַּחֲווּ לַה׳ בְּהַר הַקֹּדֶשׁ
בִּירוּשָׁלָיִם

And they shall come forth that were lost in the land of Assyria, and they that were dispersed in the land of Egypt; and they shall worship the Lord in the holy mountain of Jerusalem.

Simchu Et Y'rushalayim

Music: Y. Shapiro
Lyrics: Isaiah 66:10

Joyously

Sim - chu ___ et Y' - ru - sha - la - yim v' - gi - lu va v' -

gi - lu va kol o - ha - ve - ha kol ___ o - ha - ve - ha si - su i - ta ma - sos kol ha-

mit - ab - lim a - le - ha si - su i - ta ma - sos kol ha -

mit - ab - lim a - le - ha si - su i - ta ma - sos kol ha -

mit - ab - lim a - le - ha si - su i - ta ma - sos kol ha - mit - ab - lim a - le - ha

Sim-chu et Y'-ru-sha-la-yim v'-gi-lu va kol o-ha-ve-ha
Si-su i-ta ma-sos kol ha-mit-ab-lim a-le-ha

שִׂמְחוּ אֶת יְרוּשָׁלַיִם וְגִילוּ בָהּ כָּל אֹהֲבֶיהָ
שִׂישׂוּ אִתָּהּ מָשׂוֹשׂ כָּל הַמִּתְאַבְּלִים עָלֶיהָ

Rejoice with Jerusalem and be glad with her, all those who love her; rejoice for joy with her, all those that mourn for her.

Vayiven Uziyahu

Music: Y. Zarai
Lyrics: 2 Chronicles 26:9, 10

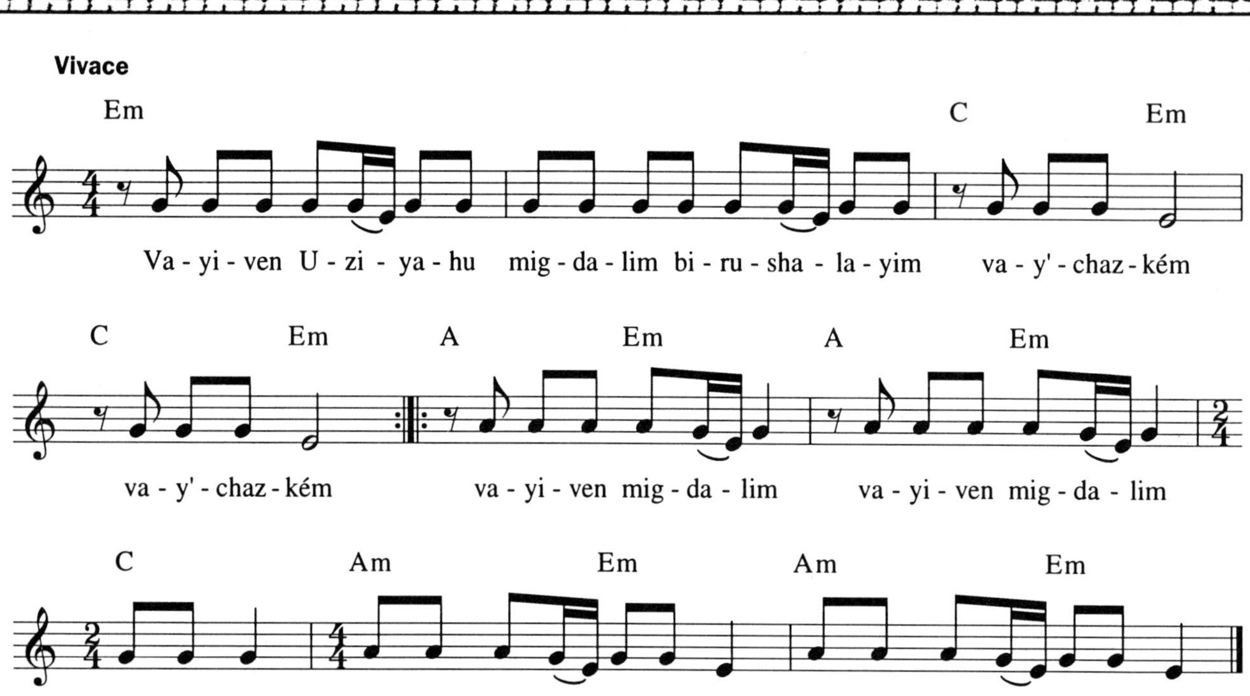

©Negen Edition

Va-yi-ven U-zi-ya-hu mig-da-lim bi-ru-sha-la-yim va-y'-chaz-kém	וַיִּבֶן עֻזִּיָּהוּ מִגְדָּלִים בִּירוּשָׁלַיִם וַיְחַזְּקֵם
Va-yi-ven mig-da-lim ba-mid-bar va-yach-tsov bo-rot ra-bim	וַיִּבֶן מִגְדָּלִים בַּמִּדְבָּר וַיַּחְצֹב בּוֹרוֹת רַבִּים

Uzziah built towers in Jerusalem and fortified them. And he built towers in the wilderness and hewed out many cisterns.

> God considered all cities throughout the world but selected only Jerusalem in which to build the holy Temple
>
> Yalkut Shimoni Habakuk

Shab'chi

Music: S. Rockoff
Lyrics: Psalm: 147:12

Allegro moderato

Dm C

Sha-b' - chi Y'-ru-sha - la-yim et Ha-shem ha-l' - li E-lo-ha-yich Tsi-

C Dm C

yon sha-b'-chi Y'-ru-sha - la-yim et Ha-shem ha-l' - li E-lo-ha-yich Tsi-

1. Dm | 2. Dm | F C7 F

yon sha-b' - yon sha-b' - chi Y' - ru - sha - la-yim__ sha-b'-

F B♭ C7 F D7 Gm F A Dm

chi Y'-ru-sha-la-yim et Ha - shem ha-l' - li Tsi-yon ha-l' - li Tsi-yon ha-l'-

1. Gm F C | 2. Gm A7 Dm

li E-lo-ha-yich Tsi - yon sha-b' - li E-lo-ha-yich Tsi - yon

© by the author

Sha-b'-chi Y'-ru-sha-la-yim et Ha-shem
Ha-l'-li E-lo-ka-yich Tsi-yon

שַׁבְּחִי יְרוּשָׁלַיִם אֶת הַ׳
הַלְלִי אֱלֹהַיִךְ צִיּוֹן

Praise the Lord O Jerusalem! Praise your God, O Zion!

Vihuda L'olam Téshév

Music: Jacobson
Lyrics: Joel

Round

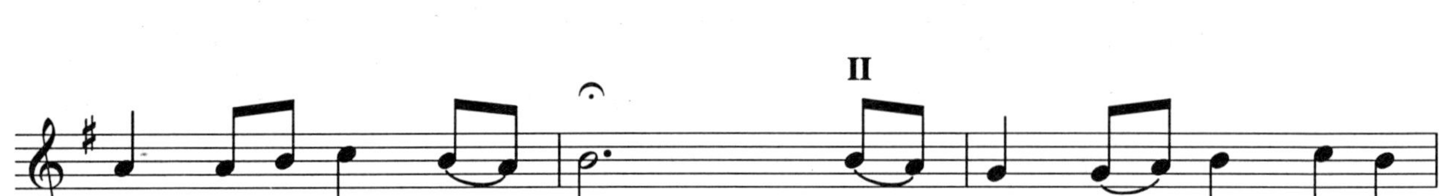

© by the author

Vi-hu-da l'-o-lam té-shév	וִיהוּדָה לְעוֹלָם תֵּשֵׁב
Vi-ru-sha-la-yim l'-dor va-dor	וִירוּשָׁלַיִם לְדוֹר וָדוֹר

The Jewish nation and Jerusalem are eternal.

V'galti Birushalayim

Music: N. Tenne
Lyrics: Isaiah

Moderately

Bi - ru - sha - la - yim bi - ru - sha - la - yim bi - ru - sha -
la - yim a - sim et shmi bi - ru - sha - la - yim a - sim et shmi v' -
gal - ti bi - ru - sha - la - yim gal - ti bi - ru - sha - la - yim gal - ti bi - ru - sha - lém v' -
sas - ti b' - a - mi v' - gal - ti bi - ru - sha - la - yim gal - ti bi - ru - sha - la - yim
gal - ti bi - ru - sha - lém v' - sas - ti b' - a - mi v' - gal - ti gal - ti gal -
- ti bi - ru - sha - lém v' - gal - ti gal - ti___ gal - ti bi - ru - sha - lém v' -
gal - ti gal - ti___ gal - ti bi - ru - sha - lém v' - sas - ti b' - a - mi

©Or-Tav Music Pub

Bi-ru-sha-la-yim a-sim et sh'-mi
V'-gal-ti bi-ru-sha-la-yim
V'-sas-ti b'-a-mi

בִּירוּשָׁלַיִם אָשִׂים אֶת שְׁמִי
וְגַלְתִּי בִּירוּשָׁלַיִם
וְשַׂשְׂתִּי בְּעַמִּי

In Jerusalem I will engrave my name. And I was joyous in Jerusalem and was happy among my people.

Im Eshkachéch

Music: S. Gewirtz
Lyrics: Psalm 137

With movement

D D7 B Em B7 Em
Im esh - ka - chéch____ Y' - ru - sha - la - yim

Em Em7 A F#m Em F
tish - kach tish - kach y' - mi - ni

D D7 B Em B7 Em
im esh - ka - chéch____ Y' - ru - sha - la - yim tish -

Bm Em F#7 Bm E Bm7
kach____ tish - kach y' - mi - ni tid - bak tid -

C D E Bm7
bak l' - sho - ni l' - chi - ki im lo im

C D F# Bm
lo ez - k' - ré - chi im lo im

G G6 F#m Bm7
lo a - a - le____ et Y' - ru - sha - la - yim im lo im

G G6 F♯m
lo a - a - le___ et Y' - ru - sha - la -

Bm Em F♯ Bm F♯
yim im lo a - a - le___ et Y' - ru - sha - la -

G Em 1. Em7 A7 D
yim al___ rosh al rosh___ sim - cha - ti___

B 2. F♯ F♯7 Bm
___ im lo im rosh___ sim - cha - ti___

© by the author

Im esh-ka-chéch Y'-ru-sha-la-yim tish-kach y'-mi-ni	אִם אֶשְׁכָּחֵךְ יְרוּשָׁלַיִם תִּשְׁכַּח יְמִינִי
Tid-bak l'-sho-ni l'-chi-ki	תִּדְבַּק לְשׁוֹנִי לְחִכִּי
Im lo ez-k'-ré-chi	אִם לֹא אֶזְכְּרֵכִי
Im lo a-a-le et Y'-ru-sha-la-yim	אִם לֹא אַעֲלֶה אֶת יְרוּשָׁלַיִם
Al rosh sim-cha-ti	עַל רֹאשׁ שִׂמְחָתִי

If I forget you, O Jerusalem, let my right hand forget her cunning. Let my tongue cleave to the roof of my mouth if I remember you not; if I set not Jerusalem above my chief joy.

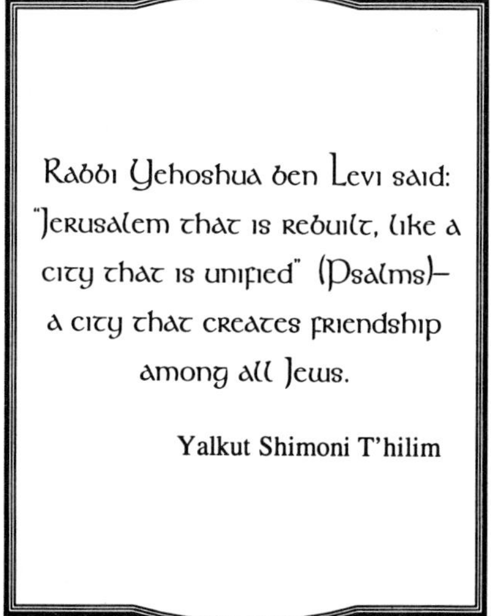

Rabbi Yehoshua ben Levi said: "Jerusalem that is rebuilt, like a city that is unified" (Psalms)— a city that creates friendship among all Jews.

Yalkut Shimoni T'hilim

Im Eshkachéch II

Music: Traditional
Lyrics: Psalm 137

Moderately

Dm Gm Dm
Im___ esh - ka - chéch___ Y'ru - sha - la - yim___

Gm Dm 1. A Dm 2. A7
tish - kach___ y' - mi - ni___ tish - kach y' - mi -

Dm A
ni___ tid - bak l' - sho - ni___ l' - chi - ki___

Dm
im___ lo___ ez - k' - ré - chi___

Gm Dm Gm
im___ lo a - a - le___ et Y'ru - sha - la - yim___ al___

A 1. A7 Dm 2. A7 Dm
rosh___ sim - cha - ti___ sim - cha - ti___

Im esh-ka-chéch Y'-ru-sha-la-yim tish-kach y'-mi-ni	אִם אֶשְׁכָּחֵךְ יְרוּשָׁלָיִם תִּשְׁכַּח יְמִינִי
Tid-bak l'-sho-ni l'-chi-ki	תִּדְבַּק לְשׁוֹנִי לְחִכִּי
Im lo ez-k'-ré-chi	אִם לֹא אֶזְכְּרֵכִי
Im lo a-a-le et Y'-ru-sha-la-yim	אִם לֹא אַעֲלֶה אֶת יְרוּשָׁלַיִם
Al rosh sim-cha-ti	עַל רֹאשׁ שִׂמְחָתִי

If I forget you, O Jerusalem, let my right hand forget her cunning. Let my tongue cleave to the roof of my mouth if I remember you not; if I set not Jerusalem above my chief joy.

Im Eshkachéch III

Music: S. Carlebach
Lyrics: Psalm 137

Moderately

Cm Fm Cm Cm Fm Cm
Im esh - ka - chéch Y' - ru - sha - la - yim tish - kach___ tish - kach tish-

F Cm Fm Cm
kach y' - mi - ni im esh - ka - chéch Y' - ru - sha - la - yim

Cm Fm Cm G7 Cm Cm
tish - kach___ tish - kach tish - kach y' - mi - ni im lo a - a - le et Y'-

Gm Fm Cm
ru - sha - la - yim al___ rosh___ sim - cha - ti im lo a - a - le et Y'-

Gm Cm
ru - sha - la - yim al rosh sim - cha - ti

© by the author

Im esh-ka-chéch Y'-ru-sha-la-yim
Tish-kach y'-mi-ni
Tid-bak l'-sho-ni l'-chi-ki
Im lo ez-k'-ré-chi
Im lo a-a-le et Y'-ru-sha-la-yim
Al rosh sim-cha-ti

אִם אֶשְׁכָּחֵךְ יְרוּשָׁלַיִם תִּשְׁכַּח יְמִינִי
תִּדְבַּק לְשׁוֹנִי לְחִכִּי
אִם לֹא אֶזְכְּרֵכִי
אִם לֹא אַעֲלֶה אֶת יְרוּשָׁלַיִם
עַל רֹאשׁ שִׂמְחָתִי

If I forget you, O Jerusalem let my right hand forget her cunning.
Let my tongue cleave to the roof of my mouth, if I remember you not: if I set not Jerusalem above my chief joy.

Uv'né Y'rushalayim

Music: S. Carlebach
Lyrics: Liturgy

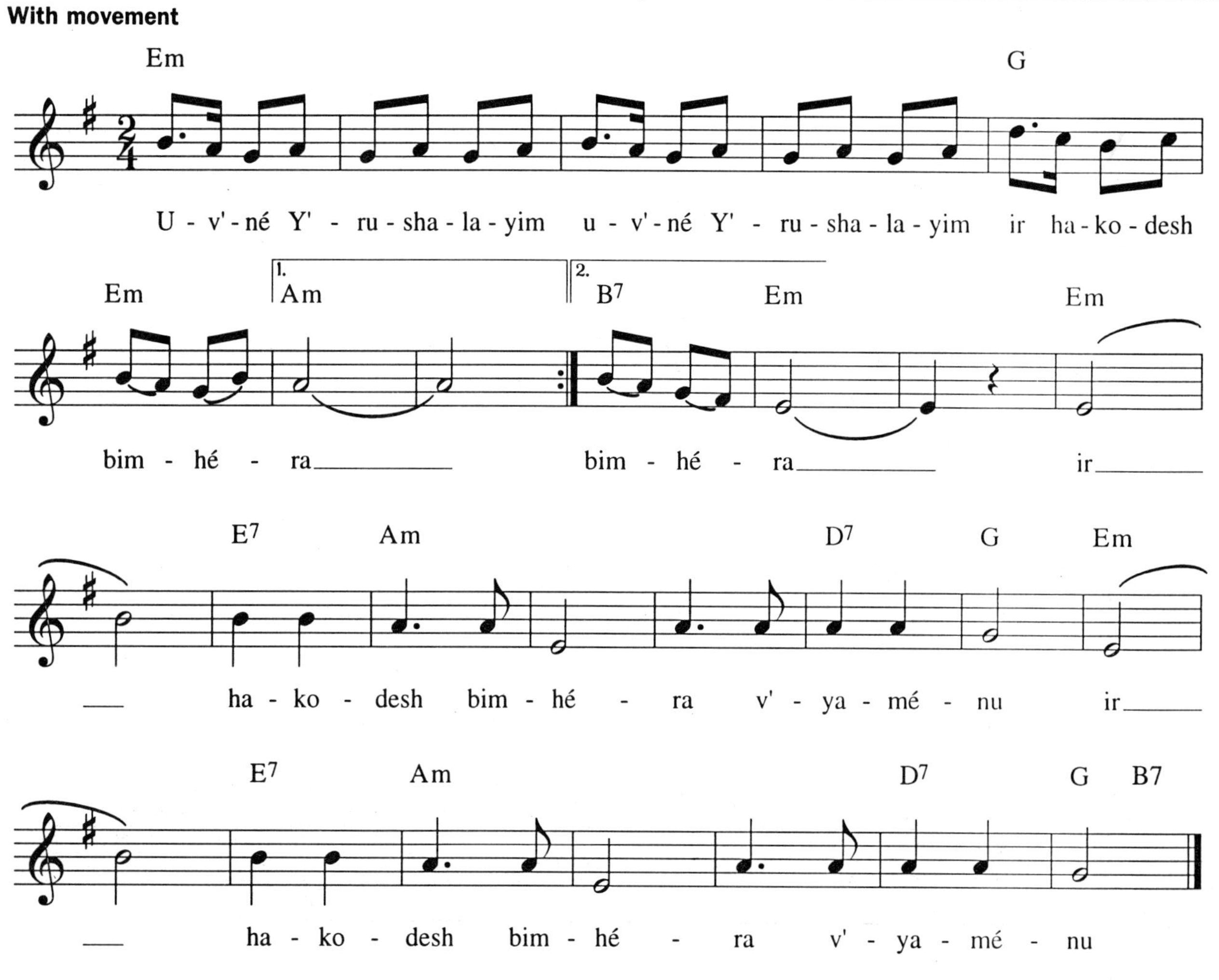

With movement

Em G
U - v' - né Y' - ru - sha - la - yim u - v' - né Y' - ru - sha - la - yim ir ha - ko - desh

Em 1. Am 2. B7 Em Em
bim - hé - ra_____ bim - hé - ra_____ ir_____

E7 Am D7 G Em
___ ha - ko - desh bim - hé - ra v' - ya - mé - nu ir_____

E7 Am D7 G B7
___ ha - ko - desh bim - hé - ra v' - ya - mé - nu

© by the author

Uv'-ne Y'ru-sha-la-yim ir ha-ko-desh bim-hé-ra v'-ya-mé-nu וּבְנֵה יְרוּשָׁלַיִם עִיר הַקֹּדֶשׁ בִּמְהֵרָה בְיָמֵינוּ

Rebuild Jerusalem, Your holy city, speedily in our days.

Uv'né Y'rushalayim II

Music: R. Sirotkin
Lyrics: Liturgy

Joyously

Dm E7 A7
Uv - né Y'-ru-sha-la-yim ir ha-ko-desh bi-m'-hé-ra v'-ya-mé-

Dm Gm
nu … né Y'-ru-sha-la-yim ir ha-ko-desh

1. Dm … sus A7 | 2. Dm A7 Dm
bi-m… nu bi-m'-hé-ra v'-ya-mé-nu uv-

Dm…
n… Uv-né Y'-ru-sha-la-yim ir ha-ko-desh bi-m'-hé-ra

Gm … C C7
v'-… né Y-ru-sha-la-yim uv-né Y'-ru-sha-la-yim

Gm7 … 1. F B♭ A7 | 2. A7 Dm
ir … -ra v'-ya-mé-nu uv- v'-ya-mé-nu

© Or-Tav Music Pub.

U-v'-né Y'-ru-sha-la-yim ir ha-ko-desh
Bim-hé-ra v'-ya-mé-nu

וּבְנֵה יְרוּשָׁלַיִם עִיר הַקֹּדֶשׁ
בִּמְהֵרָה בְיָמֵינוּ

Rebuild Jerusalem, Your holy city, speedily in our days.

Yibane Hamikdash

Music: Traditional
Lyrics: Z'mirot Liturgy

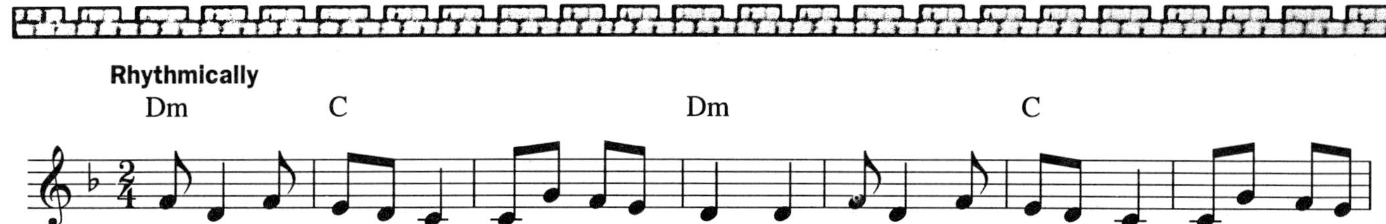

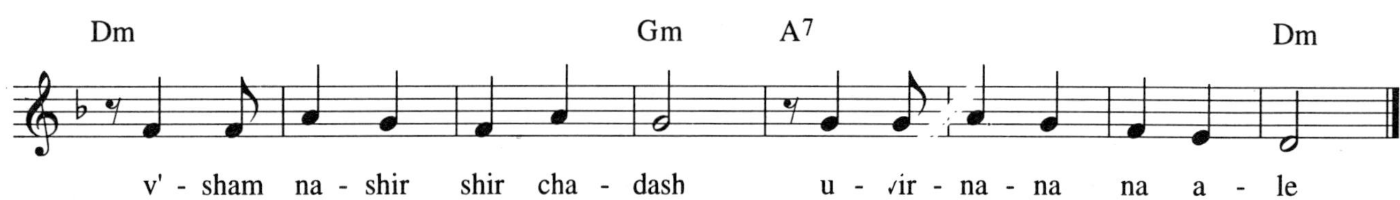

Yibane Hamikdash II

Music: Bostoner Rebbe
Lyrics: Z'mirot Liturgy

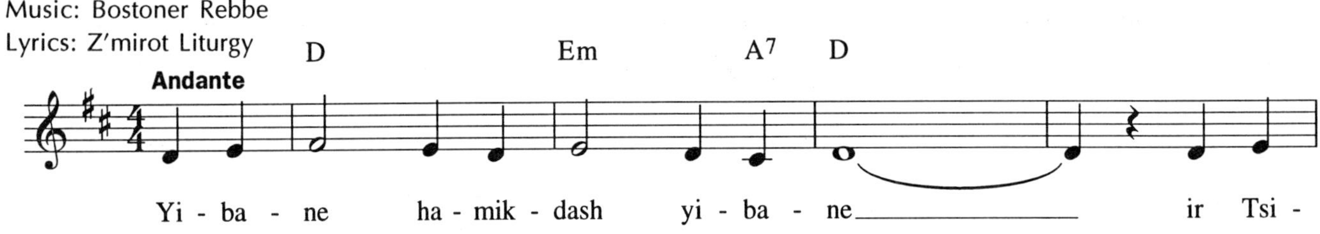

Yi-ba-ne ha-mik-dash ir tsi-yon t'-ma-lé
V'-sham na-shir shir cha-dash
U-vir-na-na na-a-le

יִבָּנֶה הַמִּקְדָּשׁ עִיר צִיּוֹן תְּמַלֵּא
וְשָׁם נָשִׁיר שִׁיר חָדָשׁ
וּבִרְנָנָה נַעֲלֶה

Let the Temple be restored, Zion refilled, that we may come up singing a new song.

Yibane Hamikdash III

Music: Folk
Lyrics: Z'mirot Liturgy

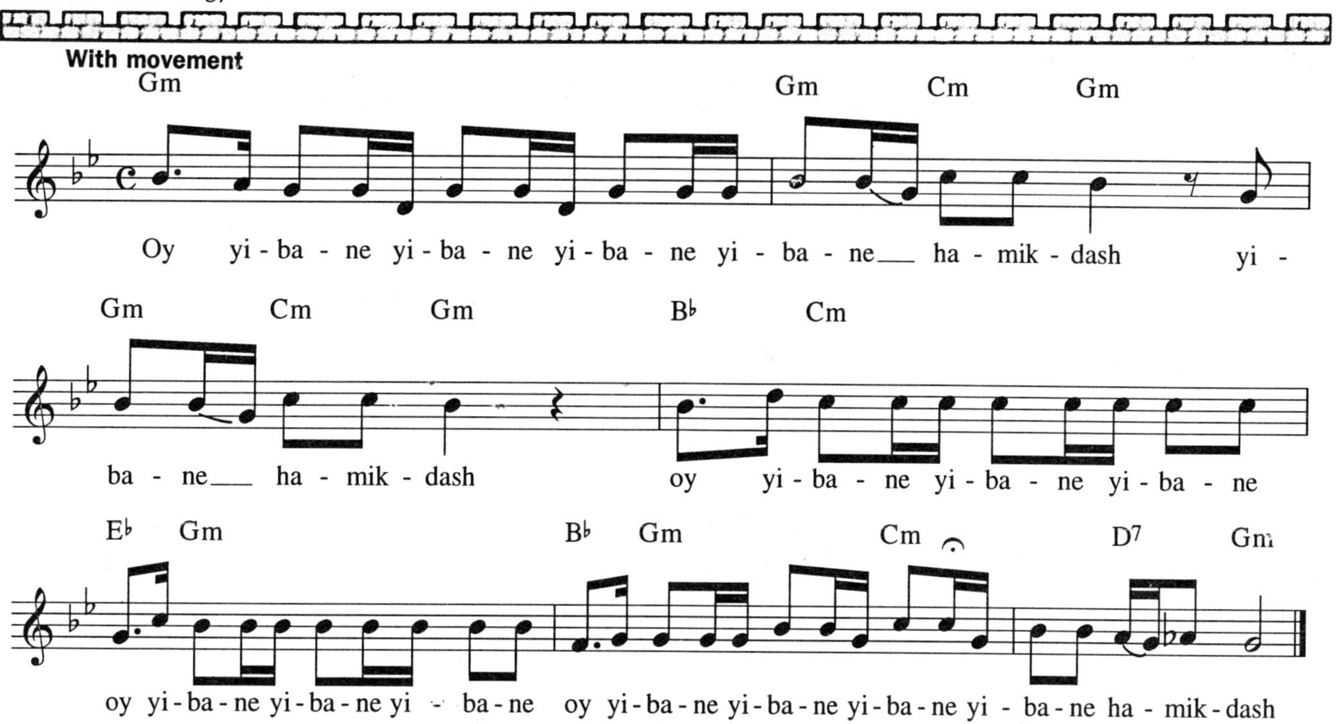

Oy yi-ba-ne ha-mik-dash	May the Temple be rebuilt.	אוֹי יִבָּנֶה הַמִּקְדָּשׁ

L'shana Haba'a

Music: S. Carlebach
Lyrics: Haggadah Liturgy

Joyously

C G7
L' - sha - na ha - ba - a bi - ru - sha - la - yim l' -

Dm G 7 C
sha - na ha - ba - a bi - ru - sha - la - yim l' - sha - na ha - ba - a

G7 Dm G7 C
bi - ru - sha - la - yim l' - sha - na ha - ba - a bi - ru - sha - la - yim l' -

Am Dm G F C
sha - na ha - ba - a bi - ru - sha - la - yim l' -

1.
Am Dm G F C
sha - na ha - ba - a bi - ru - sha - la - yim l' -

2.
C Am Dm G C
sha - na ha - ba - a bi - ru - sha - la - yim

© by the author

L'-sha-na ha-ba-a bi-ru-sha-la-yim

לְשָׁנָה הַבָּאָה בִּירוּשָׁלַיִם

Next year in Jerusalem!

L'shana Haba'a II

Music: M. Nathanson
Lyrics: Haggadah Liturgy

L'shana Haba'a III

Music: Traditional
Lyrics: Haggadah Liturgy

L'-sha-na ha-ba-a bi-ru-sha-la-yim hab-nu-ya

לְשָׁנָה הַבָּאָה בִּירוּשָׁלַיִם

Next year in Jerusalem!

L'shana Haba'a IV

Music: S. Paikov
Lyrics: Haggadah Liturgy

Allegro moderato

Dm Gm A7 Dm F
L' - sha - na ha - ba - a bi - ru - sha - la - yim l' - sha - na ha - ba - a

B♭ C7 F A7 Dm Gm A7 Dm
bi - ru - sha - la - yim l' - sha - na ha - ba - a bi - ru - sha - la - yim l' -

F B♭ C7 F D7 Gm
sha - na ha - ba - a bi - ru - sha - la - yim bi - ru - sha - la - yim

C7 F Dm Gm A
bi - ru - sha - la - yim bi - ru - sha - la - yim hab - nu - ya

D7 Gm C7 F Dm Gm A7
bi - ru - sha - la - yim bi - ru - sha - la - yim bi - ru - sha - la - yim hab - nu -

Dm Dm Gm C7 D7 Gm
ya l' - sha - na ha - ba - a bi - ru - sha - la - yim hab - nu - ya bi -

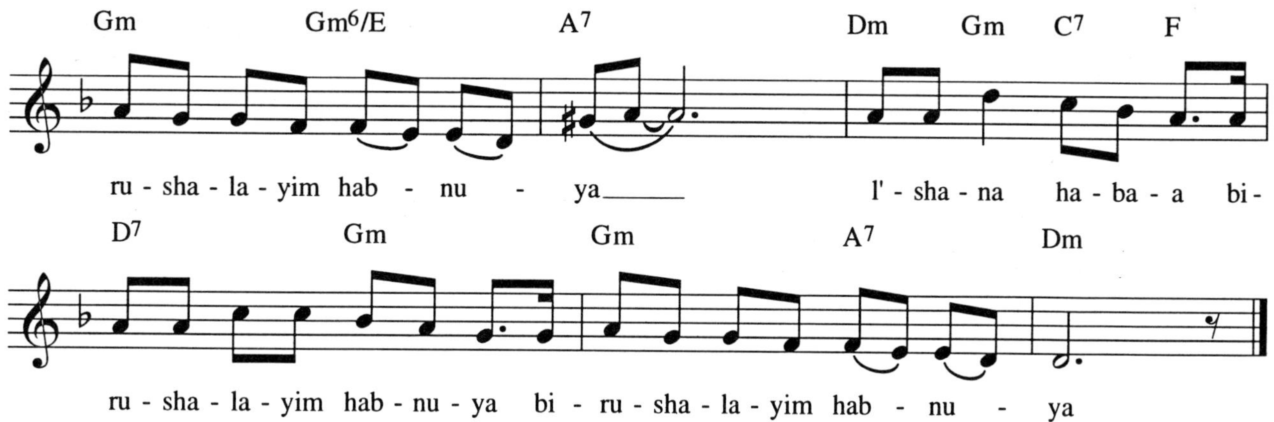

© Or-Tav Music Pub

La-sha-na ha-ba-a bi-ru-sha-la-yim hab'-nu-ya

לְשָׁנָה הַבָּאָה בִּירוּשָׁלַיִם הַבְּנוּיָה

Next year in Jerusalem the rebuilt.

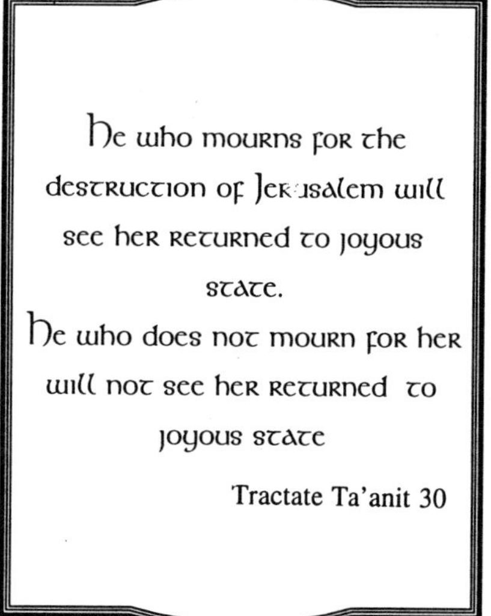

L'shana Haba'a V

Music: Traditional
Lyrics: Haggadah Liturgy

Allegro moderato

L'-sha - na ha-ba-a bi-ru-sha - la-yim hab'-nu-ya e-rets
chem-da to-va u-r'-cha - va l'-sha - va v'-ha-a-
lé - nu l'-to-cha v'-sam - ché-nu b'-vin-ya-na Y'-ru-sha-
la-yim Y'-ru-sha-la-yim hab'-nu - ya____ v'-ha-a - ya l'-sha-
na ha-ba - a bi - ru-sha - la-yim hab'-nu - ya e-rets
chem-da to-va u-r'-cha - va l'-sha - chem-da to-va u-r'-cha - va

L'-sha-na ha-ba-a bi-ru-sha-la-yim hab'-nu-ya
E-retz chem-da to-va ur'-cha-va
V'-ha-a-lé-nu l'-to-cha v'-sam-ché-nu b'-vin-ya-na

לְשָׁנָה הַבָּאָה בִּירוּשָׁלַיִם הַבְּנוּיָה
אֶרֶץ חֶמְדָּה טוֹבָה וּרְחָבָה
וְהַעֲלֵנוּ לְתוֹכָהּ וְשַׂמְּחֵנוּ בְּבִנְיָנָהּ

Next year in Jerusalem!

V'Irushalayim Ircha

Music: Dveykus
Lyrics: Liturgy

Moderately

Em | Am | Em
V' - li - ru - sha - la - yim ir - cha ___ b' - ra - cha - mim b' -

Am Em Am | Em | G Am
ra - cha - mim ___ ta - shuv v' - tish - kon b' - to - cha ka - a - sher di - bar - ta v' -

Em Am D | 1. B7 Em | 2. B7 Em
tish - kon b' - to - cha ka' - sher di - bar - ta v' - sher di - bar - ta ___

Am | Em | D7
uv - né o - ta b' - ka - rov b' - ya - mé - nu

G | Am | Em
bin - yan o - lam ___ v' - chi - sé Da - vid Da - vid av - d' - cha m' -

Am D | 1. B7 Em | 2. B7 Em
hé - ra m' - hé - ra l' - to - cha - ta - chin ___ to - cha ta -

V'-li-ru-sha-la-yim ir-cha b'-ra-cha-mim ta-shuv
V'-tish-kon b'-to-cha ka-a-sher di-bar-ta
Uv-né o-ta b'-ka-rov b'-ya-mé-nu bin-yan o-lam
V'-chi-sé Da-vid av-d'-cha m'-hé-ra l'-to-cha ta-chin

וְלִירוּשָׁלַיִם עִירְךָ בְּרַחֲמִים תָּשׁוּב
וְתִשְׁכּוֹן בְּתוֹכָהּ כַּאֲשֶׁר דִּבַּרְתָּ
וּבְנֵה אוֹתָהּ בְּקָרוֹב בְּיָמֵינוּ בִּנְיַן עוֹלָם
וְכִסֵּא דָוִד עַבְדְּךָ מְהֵרָה לְתוֹכָהּ תָּכִין

Return in mercy to your city Jerusalem and dwell in it as you have promised; rebuild it soon in our days as an everlasting structure, and speedily establish in it the throne of David.

V'Irushalayim Ircha II

Music: B.Z. Shenker
Lyrics: Liturgy

Moderately

Dm Gm A7
V'-li-ru-sha - la - yim ir - cha______ b' - ra - cha - mim ta -

Dm B♭ F
shuv______ v' - tish - kon___ b' - to - cha___ ka - a - sher di -

1. C7 F Am 2. A7 Dm Dm
bar - ta______ v'-li-ru-sha - bar - ta______ u - v' - né u - v'-

Am Gm Dm
né o - ta______ b'-ka - rov b'-ya - mé - nu______ u - v'-

B♭ F Gm F
né u - v' - né o - ta______ bin - yan o - lam______

F Dm Gm F Dm
___ v' - chi - sé______ Da - vid Da - vid av - de -

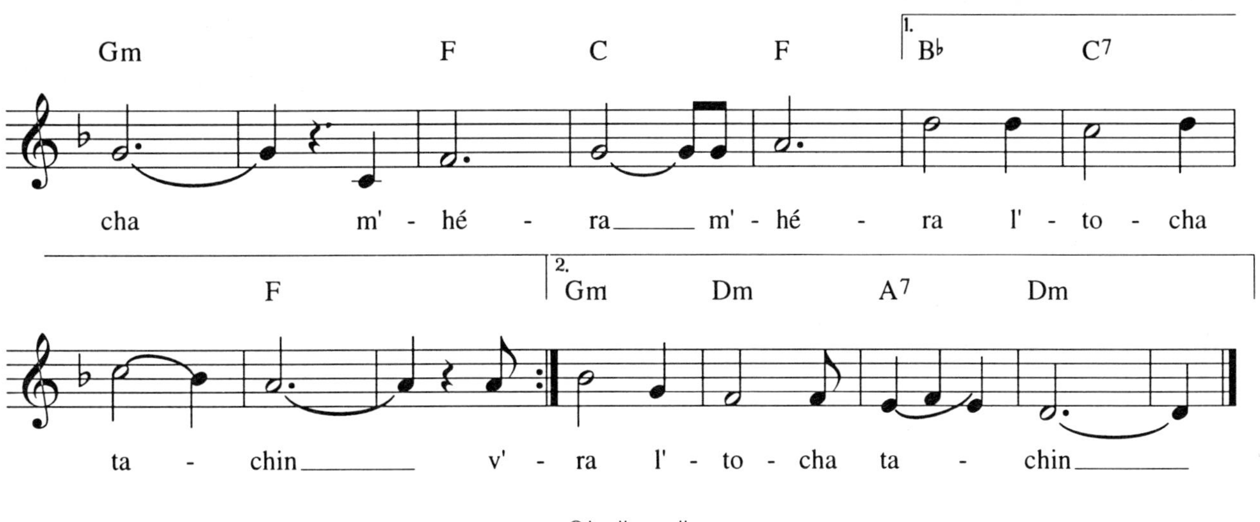

© by the author

וְלִירוּשָׁלַיִם עִירְךָ בְּרַחֲמִים תָּשׁוּב
וְתִשְׁכּוֹן בְּתוֹכָהּ כַּאֲשֶׁר דִּבַּרְתָּ
וּבְנֵה אוֹתָהּ בְּקָרוֹב בְּיָמֵינוּ בִּנְיַן עוֹלָם
וְכִסֵּא דָוִד עַבְדְּךָ מְהֵרָה לְתוֹכָהּ תָּכִין

V'-li-ru-sha-la-yim ir-cha b'-ra-cha-mim ta-shuv
V'-tish-kon b'-to-cha ka-a-sher di-bar-ta
Uv-né o-ta b'-ka-rov b'-ya-mé-nu bin-yan o-lam
V'-chi-sé Da-vid av-d'-cha m'-hé-ra l'-to-cha ta-chin

Return in mercy to your city Jerusalem and dwell in it as you have promised; rebuild it soon in our days as an everlasting structure, and speedily establish in it the throne of David.

V'Lirushalayim Ircha III

Music: S. Rockoff
Lyrics: Liturgy

Joyously

Cm G7 Cm
V' - li - ru - sha - la - yim ir - cha___ b' - ra - cha - mim ta -

G7 G7
shuv___ v' - tish - kon b' - to - cha___ ka - a - sher di -

1. Cm 2. Cm Cm G7 Cm
bar - ta___ v' - bar - ta___ u - v' - né o - ta b' - ka - rov___

Cm G7 G7
___ b' - ka - rov b' - ya - mé - nu bin - yan o - lam v' - chi - sé Da - vid m' - hé-

G7 1. Cm 2. Cm
ra___ m' - hé - ra l' - to - cha ta - chin___ u - v' - chin___

© by the author

V'-li-ru-sha-la-yim ir-cha b'-ra-cha-mim ta-shuv
V'-tishkon b'-to-cha ka-a-sher di-bar-ta
Uv-né o-ta b'-ka-rov b'-ya-mé-nu bin-yan o-lam
V'-chi-sé Da-vid m'-hé-ra l'-to-cha ta-chin

וְלִירוּשָׁלַיִם עִירְךָ בְּרַחֲמִים תָּשׁוּב
וְתִשְׁכּוֹן בְּתוֹכָהּ כַּאֲשֶׁר דִּבַּרְתָּ
וּבְנֵה אוֹתָהּ בְּקָרוֹב בְּיָמֵינוּ בִּנְיַן עוֹלָם
וְכִסֵּא דָוִד מְהֵרָה לְתוֹכָהּ תָּכִין

Return in mercy to Your city Jerusalem and dwell in it as You have promised; rebuild it soon in our days as an everlasting structure, and speedily establish in it the throne of David.

V'lirushalayim Ircha IV

Music: S. Paikov
Lyrics: Liturgy

Rhythmically

Cm Bb
V'-li-ru-sha-la-yim ir-cha___ b'-ra-cha-mim___ ta-shuv v'-

Eb Bb Eb Fm G7 Cm G7 Cm
tish-kon b'-to-cha ka-a-sher di-bar-ta___ v'-li-ru-sha-la-yim ir-cha___

Bb Eb Bb Eb Fm
b'-ra-cha-mim___ ta-shuv v'-tish-kon b'-to-cha

G7 Cm G7 Cm
ka-a-sher di-bar-ta___ uv-né uv-né uv-né___ o-ta o-ta o-ta b'-

Fm Cm Fm Cm 1. Bb7 Eb G7 2. G7 Cm
ka-rov b'-ya-mé-nu___ ya-mé-nu ya-mé-nu

© by the author

V'-li-ru-sha-la-yim ir-cha b'-ra-cha-mim ta-shuv
V'-tish-kon b'-to-cha ka-a-sher di-bar-ta
Uv-né o-ta b'-ka-rov b'-ya-mé-nu

וְלִירוּשָׁלַיִם עִירְךָ בְּרַחֲמִים תָּשׁוּב
וְתִשְׁכּוֹן בְּתוֹכָהּ כַּאֲשֶׁר דִּבַּרְתָּ
וּבְנֵה אוֹתָהּ בְּקָרוֹב בְּיָמֵינוּ

Return in mercy to Your city Jerusalem and dwell in it as You have promised; rebuild it soon in our days.

Y'rushalayim Ir Kala

A. Meller

Moderately

Gm D Gm D

Y' - ru - sha - la - yim ir ka - la kchu - lat é - na - yim

Gm D Gm D B♭

Y' - ru - sha - la - yim ir shel she - mesh uf - sa - got b' - sim - chat__ klu - lo -

F F7 Gm Gdim

ta - yich ya - ki - fuch__ kol do - da - yich bim - cho - lot ha - ma - cha -

D7 1. Gm D 2. Gm

na - yim v' - ko - lo shel tof Mir - yam v' - ko - lo shel tof Mir -

Cm Gm

yam im esh - ka - chéch__ Y' - ru - sha - la - yim im esh - ka -

D7 1. Gm 2. Gm

chéch__ tish - kach y' - mi - ni____ im esh - ka - ni

© Or-Tav Music Pub.

Y'-ru-sha-la-yim ir ka-la k'-chu-lat é-na-yim
Y'-ru-sha-la-yim ir shel she-mesh uf-sa-got
B'-sim-chat klu-lo-ta-yich
Ya-ki-fu kol do-da-yich
Bim-cho-lot ha-ma-cha-na-yim
V'-ko-lo shel tof Mir-yam
Refrain
Im esh-ka-chéch Y'-ru-sha-la-yim
Tish-kach y'-mi-ni

L'-cho-mo-ta-yich nash-ku kol gi-bo-ra-yich
Bish-vu-at tom lach l'-va-vam kash-ru
Hat-fi-la a-chat mu-na-chat
B'-kot-lo shel har ha-ba-yit
Ha-sho-me-ret yom va-lél
Et ga-che-let k'-lu-la-téch

יְרוּשָׁלַיִם עִיר כַּלָּה כְּחֻלַּת עֵינַיִם
יְרוּשָׁלַיִם עִיר שֶׁל שֶׁמֶשׁ וּפְסָגוֹת
בְּשִׂמְחַת כְּלוּלוֹתַיִךְ
יַקִּיפוּ כָּל דּוֹדַיִךְ
בִּמְחוֹלוֹת הַמַּחֲנָיִם
וְקוֹלוֹ שֶׁל תֹּף מִרְיָם
פזמון
אִם אֶשְׁכָּחֵךְ יְרוּשָׁלַיִם
תִּשְׁכַּח יְמִינִי

לְחוֹמוֹתַיִךְ נָשְׁקוּ כָּל גִּבּוֹרַיִךְ
בִּשְׁבוּעַת תֹּם לָךְ לְבָבָם קָשְׁרוּ
הַתְּפִלָּה אַחַת מֻנַּחַת
בְּכָתְלוֹ שֶׁל הַר הַבַּיִת
הַשּׁוֹמֶרֶת יוֹם וָלֵיל
אֶת גַּחֶלֶת כְּלוּלָתֵךְ *פזמון*

Jerusalem my blue-eyed bride, city of sun and hilltops. All your friends surround you at your joyous wedding in a whirling dance to the sound of Miriam's drum. "If I forget you Jerusalem may my right hand forget its cunning".

Ten measures of beauty
descended into the world
Nine were taken by Jerusalem
And the remaining one by the
rest of the world

Tractate Kidushin 49

Shiru Lanu

Music: Traditional
Lyrics: Psalm 137:3

With movement

Gm D Gm D Gm D Gm
Shi - ru la - nu mi - shir Tsi - yon shi - ru la - nu mi - shir___ Tsi - yon___

Gm D B♭ D Gm Cm D7 Gm Gm
shi - ru la - nu mi - shir Tsi - yon mi - shir___ Tsi - yon___ éch na -

Cm F Gm Cm F Gm E♭ D
shir___ éch na - shir___ éch na - shir et shir___ Ha - shem___

D Cm 1. Gm 2. Gm D
al ad - mat né - char___ char im esh - ka - chéch Y' -

D Gm Gm
ru - sha - la - yim tish - kach y' - mi - ni___ tid - bak l' - sho - ni l' -

Cm D Gm E♭
chi - ki im lo ez - k' - ré - chi im___ lo a - a - le et Y' - ru - sha - la - yim

Gm D Gm
al rosh sim - cha - ti___ tid - bak l' - sho - ni l' - chi - ki im lo ez - k' -

Shi-ru la-nu mi-shir Tsi-yon	שִׁירוּ לָנוּ מִשִּׁיר צִיּוֹן
Éch na-shir et shir Ha-shem	אֵיךְ נָשִׁיר אֶת שִׁיר ה׳
Al ad-mat né-char	עַל אַדְמַת נֵכָר
Im esh-ka-chéch Y'-ru-sha-la-yim	אִם אֶשְׁכָּחֵךְ יְרוּשָׁלַיִם תִּשְׁכַּח יְמִינִי
Tish-kach y'-mi-ni	תִּדְבַּק לְשׁוֹנִי לְחִכִּי
Tid-bak l'-sho-ni l'-chi-ki	אִם לֹא אֶזְכְּרֵכִי
Im lo ez-k'-ré-chi	אִם לֹא אַעֲלֶה אֶת יְרוּשָׁלַיִם
Im lo a-a-le et Y'-ru-sha-la-yim	עַל רֹאשׁ שִׂמְחָתִי
Al rosh sim-cha-ti	

Sing us one of the Songs of Zion. How shall we sing the Lord's song in a foreign land? If I forget you, O Jerusalem, let my right hand forget her cunning. Let my tongue cleave to the roof of my mouth if I do not remember you; if I do not set Jerusalem above my chief joy.

Rabbi Yochanan said:
Jerusalem is destined to
become a metropolis for the
entire world.

Sh'mot Raba

L'mikdashéch Tuv

Music: Traditional
Lyrics: Z'mirot Liturgy

Slowly with feeling

Dm A7 Dm A Dm Gm A7
L' - mik - da - shéch tuv___ l' - mik - da - shéch tuv___ u - l' - ko - desh kud -

Dm Gm Dm A7 Dm Dm Gm Dm
shin___ u - l' - ko - desh kud - shin___ a - tar a - tar a - tar___ a -

Dm C7 F Gm FDm A7
tar di vé yech - dun___ a - tar di vé yech - dun___ ru - chin v' - naf -

Dm B♭ C7 F Gm C7 F
shin___ vi - zam - run lach___ shi - rin v' - ra - cha - shin___

1. 2.

C7 Dm Gm Dm Gm C7 F Gm Dm Gm A7 Dm
bi - ru - sha - lém___ kar - ta d' - shuf - ra - ya___ kar - ta d' - shuf - ra - ya___

L'-mik-da-shéch tuv u-l'-ko-desh kud-shin
A-tar di vé yech-dun ru-chin v'-naf-shin
Vi-zam-run lach shi-rin v'-ra-cha-shin
Bi-rush-lém kar-ta d'-shuf-ra-ya

לְמִקְדָשֵׁךְ תּוּב וּלְקֹדֶשׁ קוּדְשִׁין
אֲתַר דִּי בֵיהּ יֶחְדוּן רוּחִין וְנַפְשִׁין
וִיזַמְרוּן לָךְ שִׁירִין וְרַחֲשִׁין
בִּירוּשְׁלֵם קַרְתָּ דְשׁוּפְרַיָא

Return to Your most holy shrine, the place where all souls will rejoice and sing hymns in Jerusalem, city of beauty.

Uvné Ota

Music: S. Carlebach
Lyrics: Liturgy

© by the author

Uv-né o-ta b'-ka-rov b'-ya-mé-nu bin-yan o-lam
V'-chi-sé Da-vid av-d'-cha m'-hé-ra l'-to-cha ta-chin

וּבְנֵה אוֹתָהּ בְּקָרוֹב בְּיָמֵינוּ בִּנְיַן עוֹלָם
וְכִסֵּא דָוִד עַבְדְּךָ מְהֵרָה לְתוֹכָהּ תָּכִין

Rebuild it soon in our days as an everlasting Temple. And speedily set up therein the throne of David, Your servant.

Ki Mitsiyon

Music: N. Shachar
Lyrics: Liturgy

Allegretto

Em Em
Ki mi - tsi - yon té - tsé To - ra ud - var Ha - shem mi -

Am B7 Em G G
ru - sha - la - yim ki mi - tsi - yon té - tsé To - ra ud - var Ha -

Am B7 1. Em 2. Em *Fine* D
shem mi - ru - sha - la - yim yim Ba - ruch she - na - tan to -

G7 C Am C D G B7 Em
ra l' - a - mo To - ra l' - a - mo Yis - ra - él ba - ruch she - na -

D D C B7 *D.S. al Fine*
tan To - ra l' - a - mo Yis - ra - él bik - du - sha - to ki mi - tsi -

© Osnat Publ. Ltd.

Ki mi-tsi-yon té-tsé To-ra
Ud-var Ha-shem mi-ru-sha-la-yim
Ba-ruch she-na-tan To-ra
L'-a-mo Yis-ra-él bik-du-sha-to

כִּי מִצִּיּוֹן תֵּצֵא תוֹרָה
וּדְבַר ה' מִירוּשָׁלָיִם
בָּרוּךְ שֶׁנָּתַן תּוֹרָה
לְעַמּוֹ יִשְׂרָאֵל בִּקְדוּשָּׁתוֹ

Truly out of Zion shall come forth the Torah, and the word of the Lord out of Jerusalem.

Ki Mitsiyon II

Music: S. Carlebach
Lyrics: Liturgy

Moderately

C C F
Ki___ mi - tsi - yon te - tsé – To - rah ud' - var Ha - shem mi -

C Am Dm
ru - sha - la - yim ki___ mi - tsi - yon té - tsé To - rah

G G7 C
ud' - var Ha - shem mi - ru - sha - la - yim ki___ mi - tsi - yon

Am Dm G G7 C
te - tsé To - rah ud' - var Ha - shem mi - ru - sha - la - yim

© by the author

Ki Mi-tsi-yon té-tsé To-ra
Ud'var Ha-shem mi-ru-sha-la-yim

כִּי מִצִּיוֹן תֵּצֵא תוֹרָה
וּדְבַר ה׳ מִירוּשָׁלָיִם

Truly out of Zion shall come forth the Torah, and the word of the Lord out of Jerusalem.

Shyibane Bét Hamikdash

Music: I. Schor
Lyrics: Liturgy

With movement

D D7 Gm

She-yi - ba - ne bét ha - mik - dash bim - hé - ra v' - ya - mé - nu v' -

Cm E♭ D

tén chel - ké - nu b' - to - ra - te - cha she - yi - ba - ne bét ha - mik - dash bim-

D7 Gm Cm D7 Cm7

hé - ra v' - ya - mé - nu v' - tén chel - ké - nu b' - to - ra - te -

D B♭ F D

Fine

cha she - yi - ba - ne bét ha - mik - dash bim - hé - ra v' - ya - mé - nu v' -

Gm E♭ D B♭

tén chel - ké - nu b' - to - ra - te - cha she - yi - ba - ne bét ha - mik - dash bim-

F D7 Gm E♭ D

D.S. al Fine

hé - ra v' - ya - mé - nu v' - tén chel - ké - nu b' - to - ra - te - cha she - yi -

She-yi-ba-ne bét ha-mik-dash
Bim-hé-ra v'-ya-mé-nu
V'-tén chel-ké-nu b'-to-ra-te-cha

שֶׁיִּבָּנֶה בֵּית הַמִּקְדָּשׁ
בִּמְהֵרָה בְיָמֵינוּ
וְתֵן חֶלְקֵנוּ בְּתוֹרָתֶךָ

May the Temple be speedily rebuilt in our days,
and grant us a share in Your Torah.

Y'varech'cha

Music: Modzitz
Lyrics: Psalm 128:5

Allegretto

Fm, B♭m
Y'-va-re-ch'-cha Ha-shem mi-tsi-yon ur'-é ur'-é b'-

1. B♭m, E♭, A♭ — tuv Y'-ru-sha-la-yim
2. B♭m, C, Fm — tuv Y'-ru-sha-la-yim

Cm
u-r'-é b'-

Fm, A♭, F7, B♭m
tuv Y'-ru-sha-la-yim kol y'-mé y'-mé cha-ye-cha

B♭m, E♭, A♭
u-r'-é b'-tuv Y'-ru-sha-la-yim kol y'-mé y'-mé cha-ye-cha

Fm, E♭
ur'-é va-nim va-nim l'-va-ne-cha

1. A♭, E♭7, A♭, B♭m — sha-lom sha-lom al Yis-ra-él
2. Fm, E♭, Fm, C7, Fm — sha-lom sha-lom al Yis-ra-él

Y'-va-re-ch'-cha Ha-shem mi-tsi-yon
U-r'-é b'-tuv Y'-ru-sha-la-yim
Kol y'-mé cha-ye-cha
Ur'-é va-nim l'-va-ne-cha
Sha-lom al Yis-ra-él

יְבָרֶכְךָ ה׳ מִצִּיּוֹן
וּרְאֵה בְּטוּב יְרוּשָׁלָיִם
כֹּל יְמֵי חַיֶּיךָ
וּרְאֵה בָנִים לְבָנֶיךָ
שָׁלוֹם עַל יִשְׂרָאֵל

The Lord bless you from Zion; may you see the welfare of Jerusalem all the days of your life; may you live to see your children's children. Peace be upon Israel.

Od Yishama

Music: B. Chait
Lyrics: Wedding Liturgy

Vivace

D D
Od___ yi-sha-ma b'-a-ré Y'-hu-da u-v'-chu-tsot___ Y'-

D
ru-sha-la-yim kol kol kol kol___ sa-son___
kol___ cha- tan___

D G
kol sa-son v'-kol___ sim-cha kol kol kol kol___ sa-son___
kol cha-tan v'-kol___ ka- la

G D
kol sa-son v'-kol sim 3 - cha kol kol kol

D A7 D
kol___ cha-tan___ kol cha-tan v'-kol___ ka-la

© by the author

Od yi-sha-ma b'-a-ré Y'-hu-da
Uv'-chu-tsot Y'-ru-sha-la-yim
Kol sa-son v'-kol sim-cha
Kol cha-tan v'-kol ka-la

עוֹד יִשָּׁמַע בְּעָרֵי יְהוּדָה
וּבְחוּצוֹת יְרוּשָׁלַיִם
קוֹל שָׂשׂוֹן וְקוֹל שִׂמְחָה
קוֹל חָתָן וְקוֹל כַּלָּה

Again may there be heard in the cities of Judah and in the streets of Jerusalem the voice of gladness, the voice of bridegroom and bride.

Od Yishama II

Music: S. Carlebach
Lyrics: Wedding Liturgy

Allegro moderato

Am Dm Am Dm
Od___ yi - sha - ma___ b' - a - ré___ Y' - hu -

Am F Dm7 Em Dm
da___ u - v' - chu - tsot u - v' - chu - tsot Y' - ru - sha -

E Am Dm
la - yim___ kol___ sa - son v' - kol sim -

E7 Am
cha___ kol___ cha - tan v' - kol ka - la___ kol___ sa -

Dm E7 Am E7 Am
son v' - kol sim - cha___ kol___ cha - tan v' - kol ka - la___

© by the author

Od yi-sha-ma b'-a-ré Y'-hu-da
Uv'-chu-tsot Y'-ru-sha-la-yim
Kol sa-son v'-kol sim-cha
Kol cha-tan v'-kol ka-la

עוֹד יִשָּׁמַע בְּעָרֵי יְהוּדָה
וּבְחוּצוֹת יְרוּשָׁלַיִם
קוֹל שָׂשׂוֹן וְקוֹל שִׂמְחָה
קוֹל חָתָן וְקוֹל כַּלָּה

Again may there be heard in the cities of Judah and in the streets of Jerusalem the voice of gladness, the voice of bridegroom and bride.

Chiko Mamtakim

Music: Traditional
Lyrics: Song of Songs

Moderately

D D A7
Chi - ko mam - ta - kim v' - chu - lo mach - ma - dim ze do -

Bm 1. Bm A 2. Bm A D Dm
di v' - ze ré - i ze ré - i ze do -

B7 Em A Em A
di v' - ze___ ré - i b' - not___ Y' - ru - sha - la - yim

Em7 D B7 Em A Em A7 D
ze do - di v' - ze___ ré - i b' - not___ Y' - ru - sha - la - yim

Chi-ko mam-ta-kim	חִכּוֹ מַמְתַּקִּים
V'-chu-lo mach-ma-dim	וְכֻלּוֹ מַחֲמַדִּים
Ze do-di v'-ze ré-i	זֶה דוֹדִי וְזֶה רֵעִי
B'-not Y'-ru-sha-la-yim	בְּנוֹת יְרוּשָׁלָיִם

His mouth is most sweet and he is altogether lovely. Such is my beloved, and such is my lover, O maidens of Jerusalem.

SONGS WITH PIANO ACCOMPANIMENT

Jerusalem of Gold

N. Shemer
Arr: C. Waldman

With Conviction

Cm Fm

A - vir ha - rim tsa - lul ka - ya - yin v' -

G C C7

ré - ach o - ra - nim ni - sa b' - ru - ach ha - ar -

Fm Cm G7 Cm Cm

ba - yim im kol pa - a - mo - nim uv′ - tar - dé - mat i - lan va -

Fm
G
C
e - ven sh'vu - ya ba - cha - lo - ma ha -
C9
Fm
Cm
G7
Cm
ir a - sher ba - dad yo - she - vet u - v' - li - ba cho - ma Y' - ru - sha -
Bb7
Eb
Ab
la - yim shel za - hav v' - shel n' - cho - shet v' - shel

©1967 by Naomi Shemer
Used by permission of CHAPPEL and Co.

A-vir ha-rim tsa-lul ka-ya-yin v'-ré-ach o-ra-nim
Ni-sa b'-ru-ach ha-ar-ba-yim im kol pa-a-mo-nim
Uv-tar-dé-mat i-lan va-e-ven sh'-vu-ya ba-cha-lo-ma
Ha-ir a-sher ba-dad yo-she-vet u-v'-li-ba cho-ma
Refrain
Y'-ru-sha-la-yim shel za-hav v'shel n'cho-shet v'shel or
Ha-lo l'chol shi-ra-yich a-ni ki-nor

אֲוִיר הָרִים צָלוּל כַּיַּיִן וְרֵיחַ אוֹרָנִים
נִישָּׂא בְּרוּחַ הָעַרְבַּיִם עִם קוֹל פַּעֲמוֹנִים
וּבְתַרְדֵּמַת אִילָן וָאֶבֶן שְׁבוּיָה בַּחֲלוֹמָהּ
הָעִיר אֲשֶׁר בָּדָד יוֹשֶׁבֶת וּבְלִבָּהּ חוֹמָה
פזמון
יְרוּשָׁלַיִם שֶׁל זָהָב וְשֶׁל נְחֹשֶׁת וְשֶׁל אוֹר
הֲלֹא לְכָל שִׁירַיִךְ אֲנִי כִּנּוֹר

Cha-zar-nu el bo-rot ha-ma-yim la-shuk v'-la-ki-kar
Sho-far ko-ré b'-har ha-ba-yit ba-ir ha-a-ti-ka
U-vam-a-rot a-sher ba-se-la al-fé shma-shot zor-chot
V'-shuv né-réd el yam ha-me-lach b'-de-rech Y'-ri-cho
Refrain

חָזַרְנוּ אֶל בּוֹרוֹת הַמַּיִם לַשּׁוּק וְלַכִּכָּר
שׁוֹפָר קוֹרֵא בְּהַר הַבַּיִת בָּעִיר הָעַתִּיקָה
וּבַמְּעָרוֹת אֲשֶׁר בַּסֶּלַע אַלְפֵי שְׁמָשׁוֹת זוֹרְחוֹת
וְשׁוּב נֵרֵד אֶל יַם הַמֶּלַח בְּדֶרֶךְ יְרִיחוֹ
פזמון

Ach b'-vo-i ha-yom la-shir lach
V'-lach lik-shor k'ta-rim
Ka-ton-ti mi-ts'-ir ba-na-yich
U-mé-a-cha-ron ha-m'-sho-r'-rim
Ki sh'-méch tso-rév et ha s'-fa-ta-yim
K'-n'-shi-kat sa-raf
Im esh-ka-chéch Y'-ru-sha-la-yim
A-sher ku-la za-hav
Refrain

אַךְ בְּבוֹאִי הַיּוֹם לָשִׁיר לָךְ
וְלָךְ לִקְשׁוֹר כְּתָרִים
קָטֹנְתִּי מִצְּעִיר בָּנַיִךְ
וּמֵאַחֲרוֹן הַמְשׁוֹרְרִים
כִּי שְׁמֵךְ צוֹרֵב אֶת הַשְּׂפָתַיִם
כִּנְשִׁיקַת שָׂרָף
אִם אֶשְׁכָּחֵךְ יְרוּשָׁלַיִם
אֲשֶׁר כֻּלָּהּ זָהָב
פזמון

Jerusalem of gold, ot copper and of light, I shall accompany all the songs dedicated to you.

NABULUS GATE

Y'rushalayim

Music: Folk
Lyrics: A. Hameiri
Arr: M. Harnik

Slowly with feeling

Dm Gm Dm A7

A7 Dm

Mé

Dm

a pis - gat___ har ha - tso - fim esh -
al pis - gat___ har ha - tso - fim sha -

A7
Dm
ta - cha - ve lach a - pa - yim mé -
lom lach Y'- ru - sha - la - yim mé -
Dm
A7
a do - rot cha - lam - ti a - la - yich liz -
f
espr.
A7
Dm
kot lir - ot b' - or pa - na - yich Y' -
Cresc.

Dm
Gm
Dm
A7
ru - sha - la - yim Y' - ru - sha - la - yim ha -
A7
Dm
i - ri fa - na - yich liv - néch
Y' -
Dm
Gm
Dm
A7
ru - sha - la - yim Y' - ru - sha - la - yim mé -

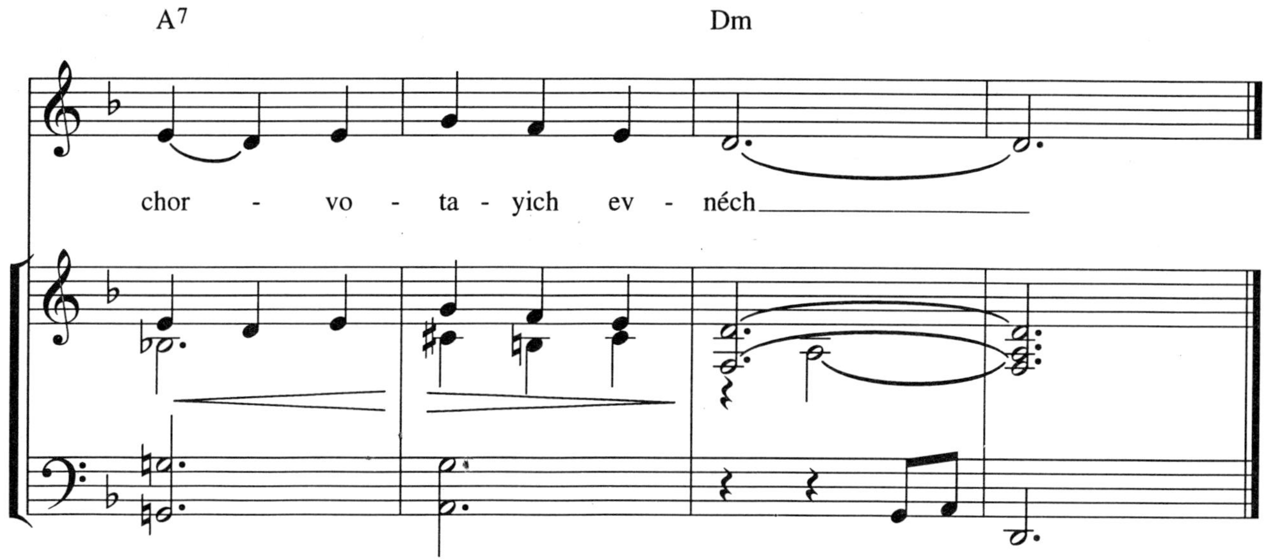

©by the author

Mé-al pis-gat har ha-tso-fim	מֵעַל פִּסְגַּת הַר הַצּוֹפִים
Esh-ta-cha-ve lach a-pa-yim	אֶשְׁתַּחֲוֶה לָךְ אַפַּיִם
Mé-al pis-gat har ha-tso-fim	מֵעַל פִּסְגַּת הַר הַצּוֹפִים
Sha-lom lach Y'-ru-sha-la-yim	שָׁלוֹם לָךְ יְרוּשָׁלַיִם
Mé-a do-rot cha-lam-ti a-la-yich	מֵאָה דוֹרוֹת חָלַמְתִּי עָלַיִךְ
Liz-kot lir-ot b'-or pa-na-yich	לִזְכּוֹת לִרְאוֹת בְּאוֹר פָּנַיִךְ
Y'-ru-sha-la-yim, Y'-ru-sha-la-yim	יְרוּשָׁלַיִם יְרוּשָׁלַיִם
Ha-i-ri pa-na-yich liv-néch	הָאִירִי פָּנַיִךְ לִבְנֵךְ
Y'-ru-sha-la-yim, Y'-ru-sha-la-yim	יְרוּשָׁלַיִם, יְרוּשָׁלַיִם
Mé-chor-vo-ta-yich ev-néch	מֵחָרְבוֹתַיִךְ אֶבְנֵךְ
Mé-al pis-gat har ha-tso-fim	מֵעַל פִּסְגַּת הַר הַצּוֹפִים
Sha-lom lach Y'-ru-sha-la-yim	שָׁלוֹם לָךְ יְרוּשָׁלַיִם
Al-fé go-lim mik-tsot kol té-vél	אַלְפֵי גוֹלִים מִקְצוֹת כָּל תֵּבֵל
Nos-im é-la-yich é-na-yim	נוֹשְׂאִים אֵלַיִךְ עֵינַיִם
B'-al-fé b'-ra-chot ha-yi v'-ru-cha	בְּאַלְפֵי בְּרָכוֹת הֲיִי בְרוּכָה
Mik-dash me-lech ir m'-lu-cha	מִקְדַּשׁ מֶלֶךְ עִיר מְלוּכָה
Y'-ru-sha-la-yim, Y'-ru-sha-la-yim	יְרוּשָׁלַיִם, יְרוּשָׁלַיִם
A-ni lo a-zuz mi-po	אֲנִי לֹא אָזוּז מִפֹּה
Y'-ru-sha-la-yim, Y'-ru-sha-la-yim	יְרוּשָׁלַיִם, יְרוּשָׁלַיִם
Ya-vo ha-ma-shi-ach ya-vo	יָבֹא הַמָּשִׁיחַ יָבֹא

From atop Mount Scopus we greet you, O Jerusalem. For a hundred generations we dreamed of your beauty. Jerusalem we shall once again rebuild you.

Y'rushalayim II

Music: M. Rapaport
Lyrics: A. Hameiri

With movement

Mé - al pis - gat har ha - tso - fim esh - ta - cha - ve lach a - pa - yim__ mé-

al pis - gat har ha - tso - fim sha - lom lach Y' - ru - sha - la - yim__ mé-

a do - rot cha - lam - ti a - la - yich liz - kot lir - ot b' - or pa na - yich Y' - ru - sha-

text see page 10

Dm C Dm C Dm
la - yim Y' - ru - sha - la - yim ha - i - ri fa - na - yich liv - néch Y' - ru - sha-
C Dm Gm F Dm
la - yim Y' - ru - sha - la - yim mé - chor - vo - ta - yich ev - néch ev - néch
Mé - al pis - gat har ha - tso - fim sha - lom lach Y' - ru - sha - la - yim al -

©Negen Edition

Im Eshkachéch IV

Music: D. Bagley
Lyrics: Psalm 137
Arr: C. Winternitz

With Feeling

Im esh - ka - chéch Y' -

ru - sha - la - yim tish - kach y' - mi -

p

ni
im esh - ka - chéch Y' -
ru - sha - la - yim tish - kach y' - mi -
ni
im esh - ka - chéch Y' -
ru - sha - la - yim tish - kach y' -

mi - ni
im esh - ka - chéch Y' - ru - sha - la - yim
tish - kach y' - mi - ni tid -
bak l' - sho - ni l' - chi - ki im

lo ez - k' - ré - chi
im lo a - a - le et Y' - ru - sha -
la - yim al rosh sim - cha -
ti
f

R.H.
L.H.
L.H.
tid - bak l' - sho - ni l' - chi - ki

Im esh-ka-chéch Y'-ru-sha-la-yim tish-kach y'-mi-ni
Tid-bak l'-sho-ni l'-chi-ki
Im lo ez-k'-ré-chi
Im lo a-a-le et Y'-ru-sha-la-yim
Al rosh sim-cha-ti

אִם אֶשְׁכָּחֵךְ יְרוּשָׁלָיִם תִּשְׁכַּח יְמִינִי
תִּדְבַּק לְשׁוֹנִי לְחִכִּי
אִם לֹא אֶזְכְּרֵכִי
אִם לֹא אַעֲלֶה אֶת יְרוּשָׁלַיִם
עַל רֹאשׁ שִׂמְחָתִי

If I forget you, O Jerusalem let my right hand forget her cunning. Let my tongue cleave to the roof of my mouth, if I remember you not: if I set not Jerusalem above my chief joy.

Od Yishama III

Music: S. Carlebach
Lyrics: Wedding Liturgy
Arr: A. Rozin

Joyously

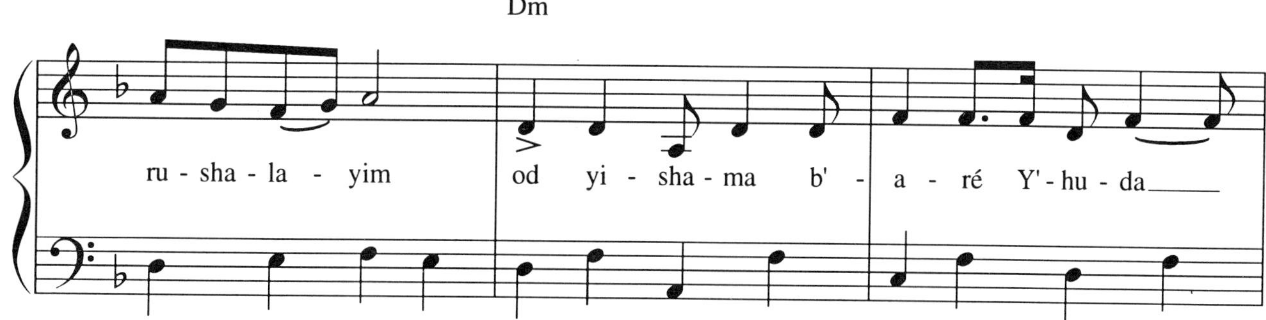

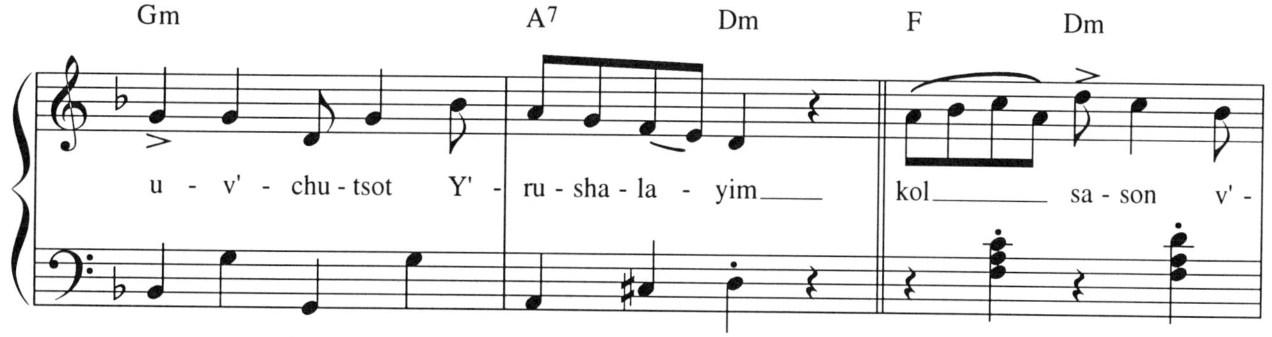

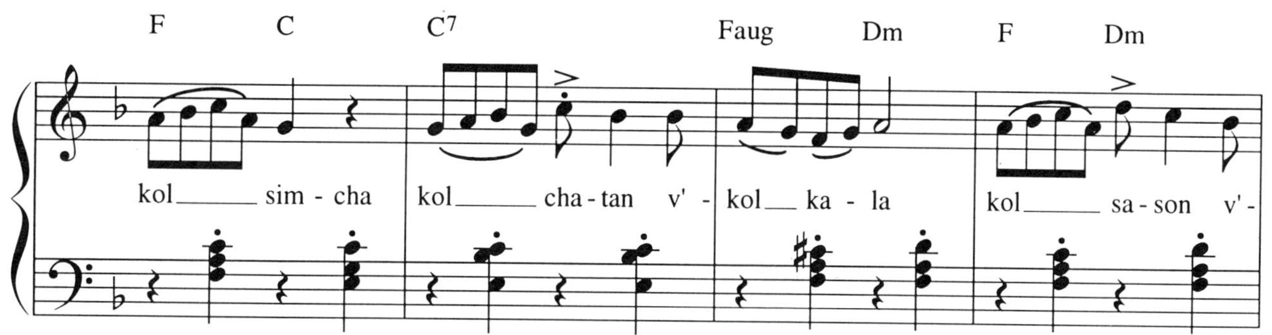

F C C7 A7 Dm
kol___ sim - cha kol___ cha - tan v' - kol___ ka - la___
Dm Gm Dm A
od yi - sha - ma b' - a - ré Y' - hu - da___ u - v - chu - tsot Y' - ru - sha - la - yim
Dm Gm
od yi - sha - ma b' - a - ré Y' - hu - da___ u - v' - chu - tsot Y' -
A7 Dm F Dm F C
ru - sha - la - yim___ kol___ sa - son v' - kol___ sim - cha

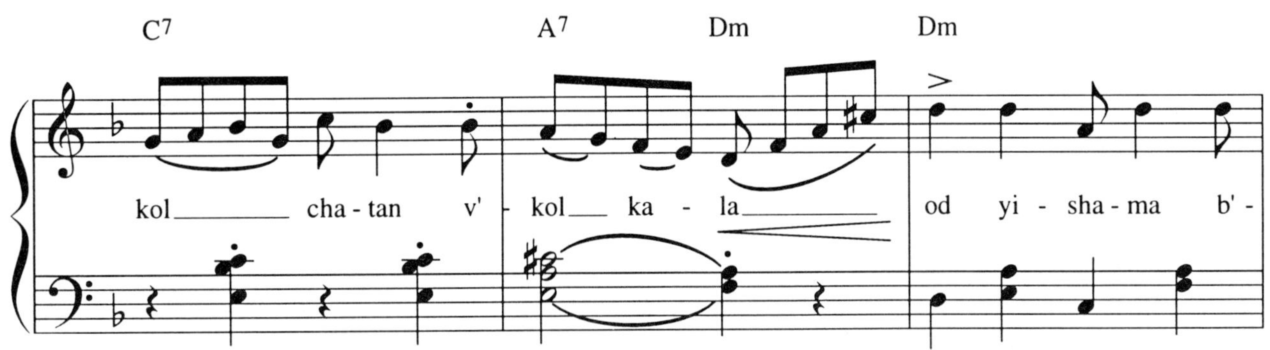

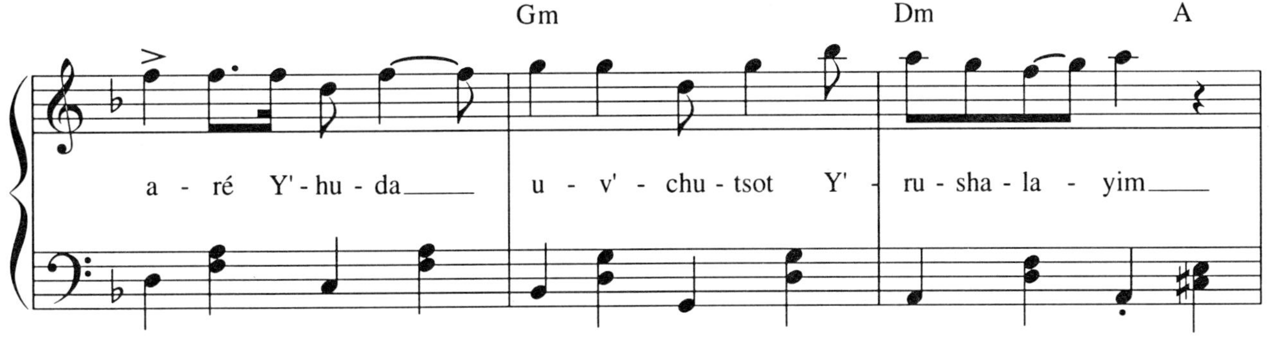

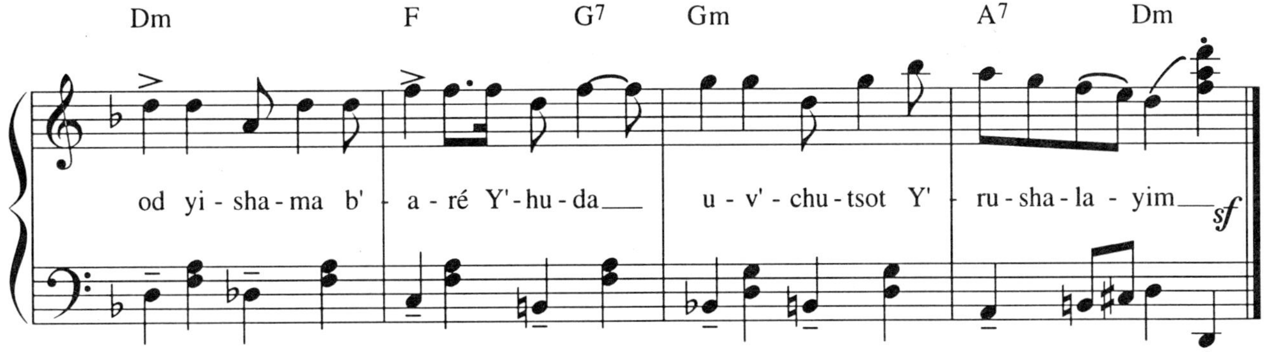

© by the author

Od yi-sha-ma b'-a-ré Y'-hu-da
Uv'-chu-tsot Y'-ru-sha-la-yim
Kol sa-son v'-kol sim-cha
Kol cha-tan v'-kol ka-la

עוֹד יִשָּׁמַע בְּעָרֵי יְהוּדָה
וּבְחוּצוֹת יְרוּשָׁלַיִם
קוֹל שָׂשׂוֹן וְקוֹל שִׂמְחָה
קוֹל חָתָן וְקוֹל כַּלָּה

Again may there be heard in the cities of Judah and in the streets of Jerusalem the voice of gladness, the voice of bridegroom and bride.

Od Yishama IV

Music: Traditional
Lyrics: Liturgy
Arr: A. Rozin

Joyously

Gm Cm Gm C

Od___ yi - sha - ma b' - a - ré Y' - hu - da u - v' - chu - tsot Y' - ru - sha - la - yim

Cm Gm Edim E♭ Gm D7 Gm

kol___ sa - son v' - kol______ sim - cha kol___ cha - tan v' - kol ka - la

Gm B♭ F7 Gm B♭ Gm F B♭

od yi - sha - ma b' - a - ré Y' - hu - da u - v' - chu - tsot Y' - ru - sha - la - yim

melody melody

Gm B♭ F7 B♭ Gm D7 Gm

kol______ sa - son v' - kol___ sim - cha kol cha - tan v' - kol___ ka - la

melody melody

Od yi-sha-ma b'-a-ré Y'-hu-da
Uv'-chu-tsot Y'-ru-sha-la-yim
Kol sa-son v'-kol sim-cha
Kol cha-tan v'-kol ka-la

עוד יִשָּׁמַע בְּעָרֵי יְהוּדָה
וּבְחוּצוֹת יְרוּשָׁלַיִם
קוֹל שָׂשׂוֹן וְקוֹל שִׂמְחָה
קוֹל חָתָן וְקוֹל כַּלָּה

Again may there be heard in the cities of Judah and in the streets of Jerusalem the voice of gladness, the voice of bridegroom and bride.

Y'varech'cha II

Music: D. Weinkranz
Lyrics: Psalm 128:5
Arr: S. Feigin

Joyously

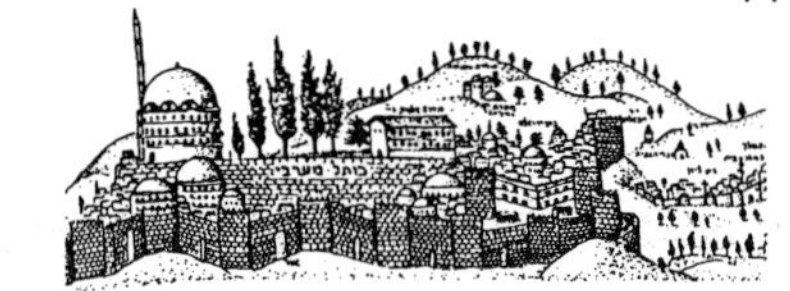

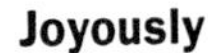

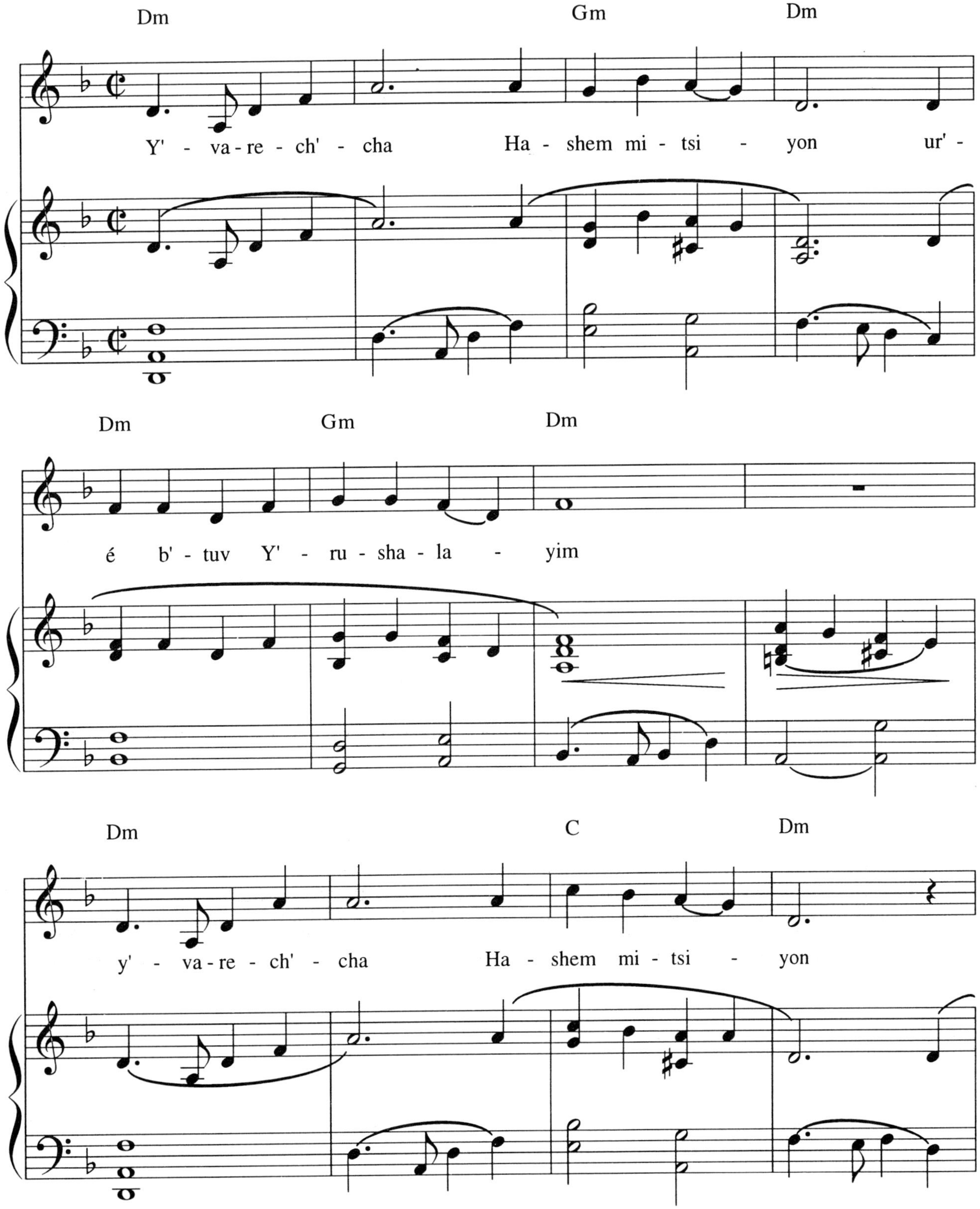
Dm
Gm
Dm
Y' - va - re - ch' - cha Ha - shem mi - tsi - yon ur' -
Dm
Gm
Dm
é b' - tuv Y' - ru - sha - la - yim
Dm
C
Dm
y' - va - re - ch' - cha Ha - shem mi - tsi - yon

Dm
A7
Dm
kol y' - mé y' - mé cha - ye - ha
Dm
D7
ur' - é va - nim l' - va - ne -
Gm
C7
F
cha sha - lom al Yis - ra - él

Dm D7 Gm

__ ur' - é__ va - nim__ l' - va -

Dm 1. C7 F

ne - cha sha - lom al Yis - ra - él__

2. A7 Dm

__ al Yis - ra - él__

©by Osnat Publ. Ltd.

Y'-va-re-ch'-cha Ha-shem mi-tsi-yon	יְבָרֶכְךָ ה׳ מִצִּיּוֹן
Ur'-é b'-tuv Y'-ru-sha-la-yim	וּרְאֵה בְּטוּב יְרוּשָׁלָיִם
Kol y'-mé cha-ye-cha	כֹּל יְמֵי חַיֶּיךָ
Ur'-é va-nim l'-va-ne-cha	וּרְאֵה בָנִים לְבָנֶיךָ
Sha-lom al Yis-ra-él	שָׁלוֹם עַל יִשְׂרָאֵל

The Lord bless you from Zion; may you see the welfare of Jerusalem all the days of your life; may you live to see your children's children. Peace be upon Israel.

Shir Ha'avoda

Music: N. Nardi
Lyrics: N. Alterman
Arr: M. Helfman

Lyrically

Em Am

Ka - chol yam ha -

mp *legato*

Em Bm7 Em

ma - yim na - va Y' - ru - sha - la - yim o -

Em Am Em Am6 Bm7

rim ha - sha - ma - yim al ne - gev v' - ga -

Em
(D)
G
D
G
lil ha - she - mesh o - ri la - nu o - ri ha - mach - ré -
mf
G
Am
Em
(D)
G
D
sha iv - ri a - vo - ri chir - shi ba - te - lem va - cha -
G
Am
Em
Bm7
Em
zo - ri ad lai - la lél yа - a - fil

© by the author

Ka-chol yam ha-ma-yim
Na-va Y'-ru-sha-la-yim
O-rim ha-sha-ma-yim
Al ne-gev v'-ga-lil
Ha-she-mesh o-ri la-nu o-ri
Ha-mach-ré-sha iv-ri a-vo-ri
Chir-shi ba-te-lem va-cha-zo-ri
Ad lai-la lél ya-a-fil
Shir shir a-lé-na
Ba-pa-ti-shim na-gén na-gé-na
Ba-mach-ré-shot ra-né-na
Ha-shir lo tam
Hu rak mat-chil

כָּחוֹל יַם הַמַּיִם
נָאוָה יְרוּשָׁלַיִם
אוֹרִים הַשָּׁמַיִם
עַל נֶגֶב וְגָלִיל
הַשֶּׁמֶשׁ אוֹרִי לָנוּ אוֹרִי
הַמַּחֲרֵשָׁה עִבְרִי עֲבֹרִי
חִרְשִׁי בַּתֶּלֶם וַחֲזֹרִי
עַד לַיְלָה לֵיל יַאֲפִיל
שִׁיר שִׁיר עֲלֵה נָא
בַּפַּטִּשִׁים נַגֵּן נַגְּנָה
בַּמַּחֲרֵשׁוֹת רַנֵּנָה
הַשִּׁיר לֹא תַּם
הוּא רַק מַתְחִיל

The workers in the field sing of the splendor of Israel to the beat of the hammer and the rhythm of the plow. Lift up your voices—"The song is not yet finished; it has only just begun."

Sisu Et Y'rushalayim

Music: A. Nof
Lyrics: Isaiah
Arr: C. Waldman

Joyously

C7 Fm B♭

Si - su et Y' - ru - sha - la - yim gi - lu va___ gi - lu va kol o - ha - ve - ha

E♭ G C7 Fm

kol___ o - ha - ve - ha si - su et Y' - ru - sha - la - yim gi - lu va___

G7 1. Cm 2. Cm

gi - lu va___ kol o - ha - ve - ha o - ha - ve - ha ve - ha

Fine

© by the author

Refrain
Si-su et Y'-ru-sha-la-yim
Gi-lu va kol o-ha-ve-ha

Al cho-mo-ta-yich ir Da-vid hif-ka-d'-ti shom-rim
Kol ha-yom v'-chol ha-lai-la *Sisu.......*

פזמון
שִׂישׂוּ אֶת יְרוּשָׁלַיִם גִּילוּ בָהּ
גִּילוּ בָהּ כָּל אוֹהֲבֶיהָ

עַל חוֹמוֹתַיִךְ עִיר דָּוִד הִפְקַדְתִּי שׁוֹמְרִים
כָּל הַיּוֹם וְכָל הַלַּיְלָה פזמון

Rejoice with Jerusalem all you who love her. I have set watchmen upon your walls, O Jerusalem. They shall never hold their peace, day or night.

Additional text see page 187

Kirya Y'féfiya

Folktune

Arr: R. Neumann

Kir-ya y'-fé-fi-ya ma-sos l'-a-ra-yich
Ir ne-e-ma-na at l'-mal-kéch v'-sa-ra-yich

קִרְיָה יְפֵהפִיָּה מָשׂוֹשׂ לְעָרַיִךְ
עִיר נֶאֱמָנָה אַתְּ לְמַלְכֵּךְ וְשָׂרַיִךְ

O beautiful city, joy of all cities, you are faithful to your king and ministers.

CHORAL ARRANGEMENTS

Al Chomotayich

Music: N. Hirsh
Lyrics: Isaiah
Arr: C. Goldberg

Spirited

Ah__ Y' - ru - sha - la - yim kol__ ha -
Al cho - mo - ta - yich Y' - ru - sha - la - yim hif - ka - d' - ti shom - rim kol ha -

yom v' - chol ha - lai - la Ah__ Y' - ru - sha -
yom v' - chol ha - lai - la__ al cho - mo - ta - yich Y' - ru - sha - la - yim hif -

la - yim yom v' - chol ha - lai - la ah______
ka - d' - ti shom - rim kol ha - yom v' - chol ha - lai - la__ ah

Y' - ru - sha - la - yim ah______ Y' - ru - sha - la - yim__
Y' - ru - sha - la - yim ah Y' - ru - sha - la - yim__

© by the author

Al cho-mo-ta-yich Y'-ru-sha-la-yim
Hif-ka-d'-ti shom-rim
Kol hayom v'-chol ha-lai-la

עַל חוֹמוֹתַיִךְ יְרוּשָׁלַיִם
הִפְקַדְתִּי שׁוֹמְרִים
כָּל הַיּוֹם וְכָל הַלַּיְלָה

I have set watchmen upon your walls, O Jerusalem. They shall never hold their peace, day or night.

L'ma'an Tsiyon

Music S. Rockoff
Lyrics: Isaiah 62:1
Arr: C. Goldberg

Joyously

* I

B♭ E♭ B♭

L' - ma'an Tsi - yon l' - ma' - an Tsi - yon lo lo lo lo

L' - ma'an Tsi - yon lo lo lo lo e - che -

Cm F B♭ E♭

lo e - che - she l' - ma'an Tsi - yon l' - ma'an Tsi - yon

she l' - ma'an Tsi - yon l' - ma'an Tsi - yon

B♭ C7 F7 II B♭

lo lo lo e - che - she u - l' - ma - an Y' - ru - sha -

lo lo lo e - che - she u - l' - ma - an Y' -

E♭ B♭ C7 F

la - yim lo lo lo esh - kot u - l' -

ru - sha - la - yim lo lo lo lo lo esh - kot u - l' -

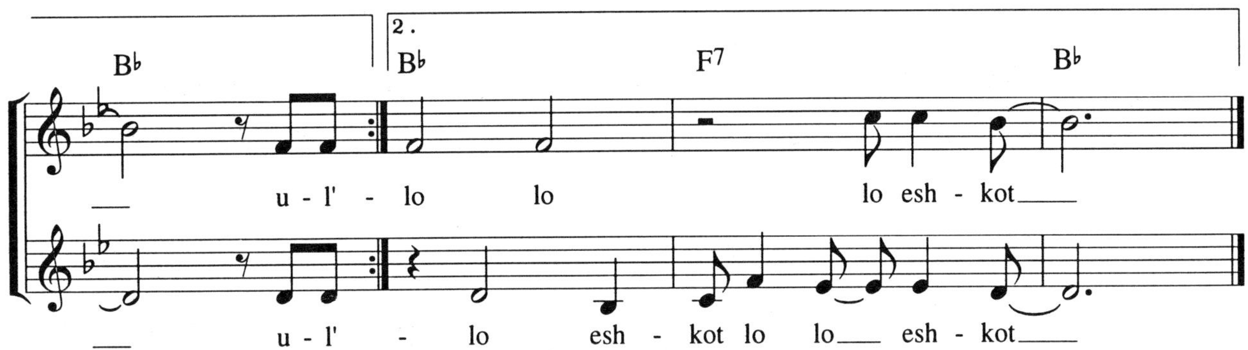

* Melody can also be sung as a round

© by the author

L'-ma-an Tsi-yon lo e-che-she
U-l'-ma-an Y'-ru-sha-la-yim lo esh-kot

לְמַעַן צִיּוֹן לֹא אֶחֱשֶׁה
וּלְמַעַן יְרוּשָׁלַיִם לֹא אֶשְׁקוֹט

For Zion's sake will I not hold my peace. And for Jerusalem's sake I will not rest.

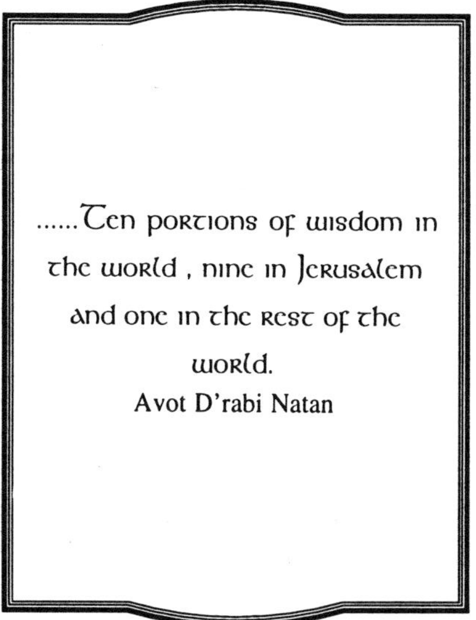

L'ma'an Tsiyon II

Music: D. Havkin
Lyrics: Isaiah 62:1
Arr: V. Pasternak

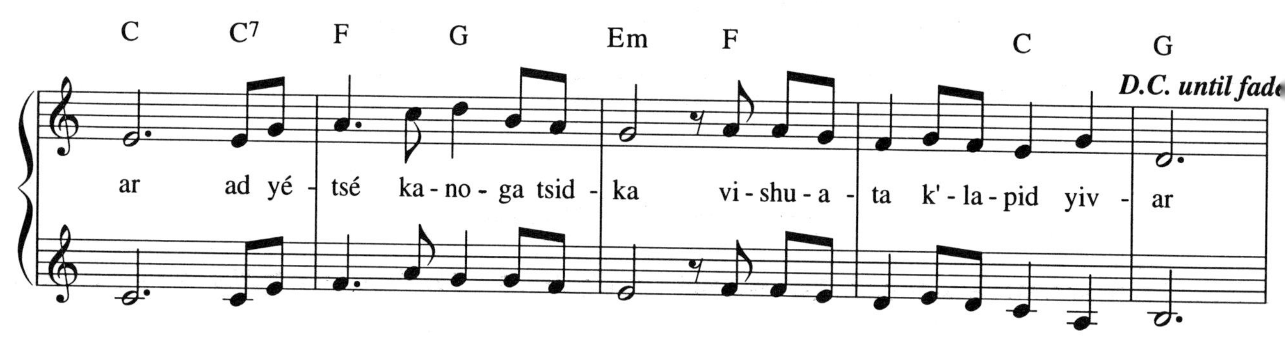

© by the author

L'-ma-an Tsi-yon lo e-che-she
Ul'-ma-an Y'-ru-sha-la-yim lo esh-kot
Ad yé-tsé ka-no-ga tsid-ka
Vi-shu-a-ta k'-la-pid yiv-ar

לְמַעַן צִיּוֹן לֹא אֶחֱשֶׁה
וּלְמַעַן יְרוּשָׁלַיִם לֹא אֶשְׁקוֹט
עַד יֵצֵא כַנֹּגַהּ צִדְקָהּ
וִישׁוּעָתָהּ כְּלַפִּיד יִבְעָר

For Zion's sake will I not hold my peace. And for Jerusalem's sake I will not rest until her triumph goes forth as brightness, and her salvation as a torch that burns.

Shalom Shuvcha Hakotel

Music: C. Najman
Lyrics: E. Indelman

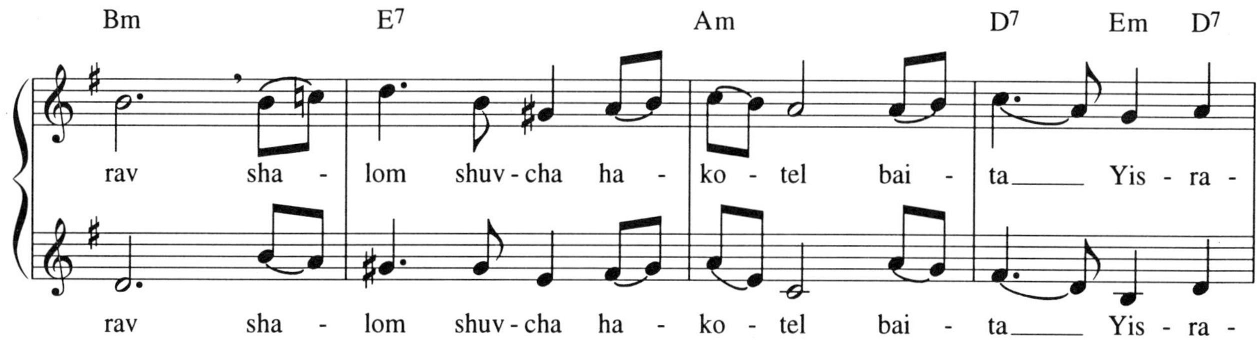

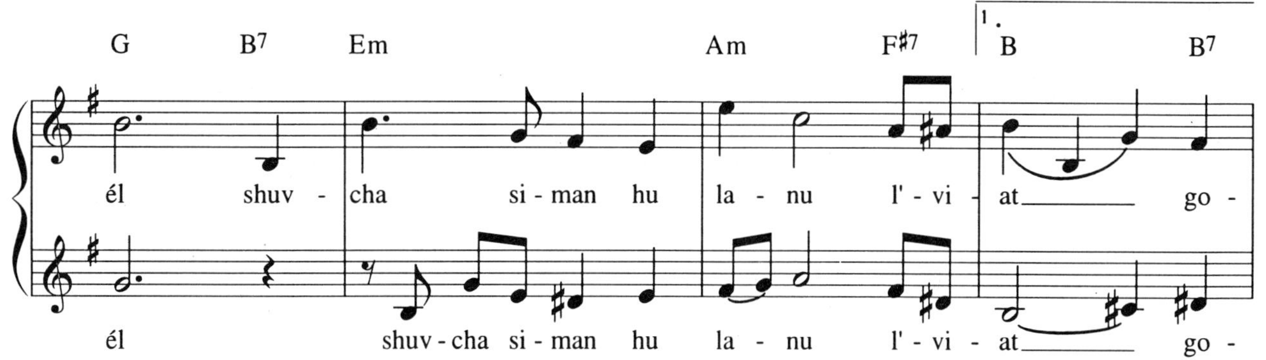

last time
Em B B7 Em Fine
él at go - él mé -
él at l' - vi - at go - él mé -

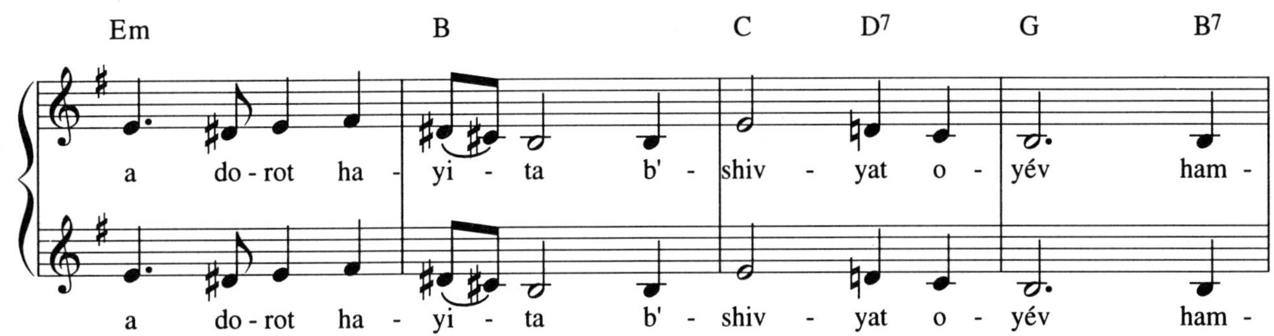
Em B C D7 G B7
a do - rot ha - yi - ta b' - shiv - yat o - yév ham -
a do - rot ha - yi - ta b' - shiv - yat o - yév ham -

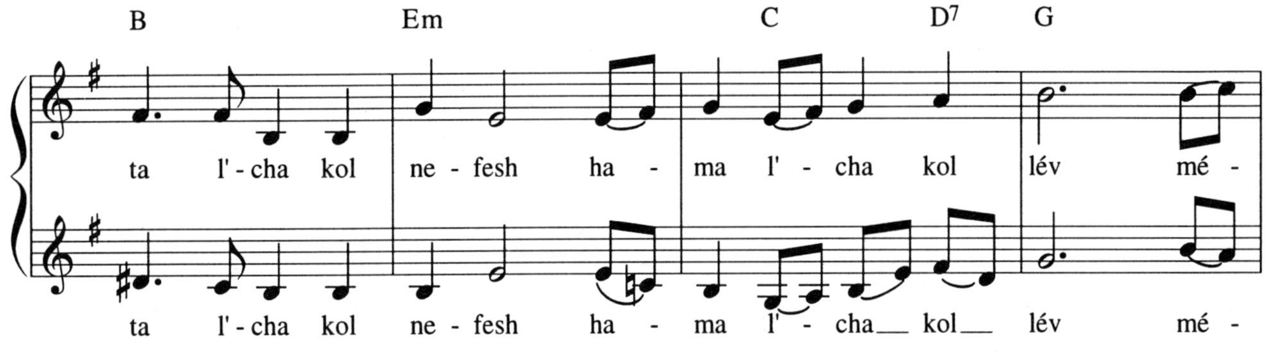
B Em C D7 G
ta l' - cha kol ne - fesh ha - ma l' - cha kol lév mé -
ta l' - cha kol ne - fesh ha - ma l' - cha kol lév mé -

E7 Dm E E7 Am
a do - rot ha - yi - ta éd l' - yam d' - ma - ot a -
a do - rot ha - yi - ta éd l' - yam d' - ma - ot d' - ma - ot a -

©by the authors

Shalom shuv-cha ha-ko-tel, ko-tel ma-a-rav
Shalom shuv-cha é-lé-nu mi-shil-ton a-rav
Shalom shuv-cha ha-ko-tel bai-ta Yis-ra-él
Shuv-cha si-man hu la-nu l'-vi-at go-él
Mé-a do-rot ha-yi-ta b'-shiv-yat o-yév
Ham-ta l'-cha kol ne-fesh ha-ma l'-cha kol lév
Mé-a do-rot ha-yi-ta éd l'-yam d'-ma-ot
A-ta lig-vu-ro-té-nu éd u-l'-nif-la-ot

שָׁלוֹם שׁוּבְךָ הַכֹּתֶל, כֹּתֶל מַעֲרָב
שָׁלוֹם שׁוּבְךָ אֵלֵינוּ מִשִּׁלְטוֹן עֲרָב
שָׁלוֹם שׁוּבְךָ הַכֹּתֶל בַּיְתָה יִשְׂרָאֵל
שׁוּבְךָ סִימָן הוּא לָנוּ לְבִיאַת גּוֹאֵל
מֵאָה דוֹרוֹת הָיִיתָ בְּשִׁבְיַת אוֹיֵב
הָמְתָה לְךָ כָּל נֶפֶשׁ הָמָה לְךָ כָּל לֵב
מֵאָה דוֹרוֹת הָיִיתָ עֵד לְיָם דְמָעוֹת
עַתָּה לִגְבוּרוֹתֵינוּ עֵד וּלְנִפְלָאוֹת

We greet you, O Western Wall, upon your return to the Jewish people. For a hundred generations every heart and soul has longed for your return. Now after all our tears you are once again ours.

Uva'ir Y'rushalayim

Music: Folk
Lyrics: Yehuda Halevi

Moderately

Dm Gm Dm Gm

U - va - ir Y' - ru - sha - la - yim yésh___ sha - ar
Al mish - mar - to___ ze al - pa - yim hu___ ni - tsav___

U - va - ir Y' - ru - sha - la - yim yésh sha - ar
mish - mar - to___ ze al - pa - yim hu ni - tsav___

Am Dm Dm Gm C7 F

shel___ za - hav u - mal - ach min ha - sha - ma - yim
yom___ va - lél ad___ ta - shuv Y' - ru - sha - la - yim

shel za - hav u - mal - ach min ha - sha - ma - yim
yom va - lél ad ta - shuv Y' - ru - sha - la - yim

C C7 F Dm Gm

ba - sha - ar lo ni - tsav u - mal - ach min
ad___ ta - shuv v' - ti - ga - él ad___ ta - shuv Y' -

ba - sha - ar lo ni - tsav (melody) u - mal - ach min
ad___ ta - shuv v' - ti - ga - él ad___ ta - shuv Y' -

C Dm Gm C Dm

ha - sha - ma - yim ba - sha - ar lo ni - tsav u - mal -
ru - sha - la - yim ad___ ta - shuv v' - ti - ga - él ad___ ta -

ha - sha - ma - yim ba - sha - ar lo ni - tsav u - mal -
ru - sha - la - yim ad___ ta - shuv v' - ti - ga - él ad___ ta -

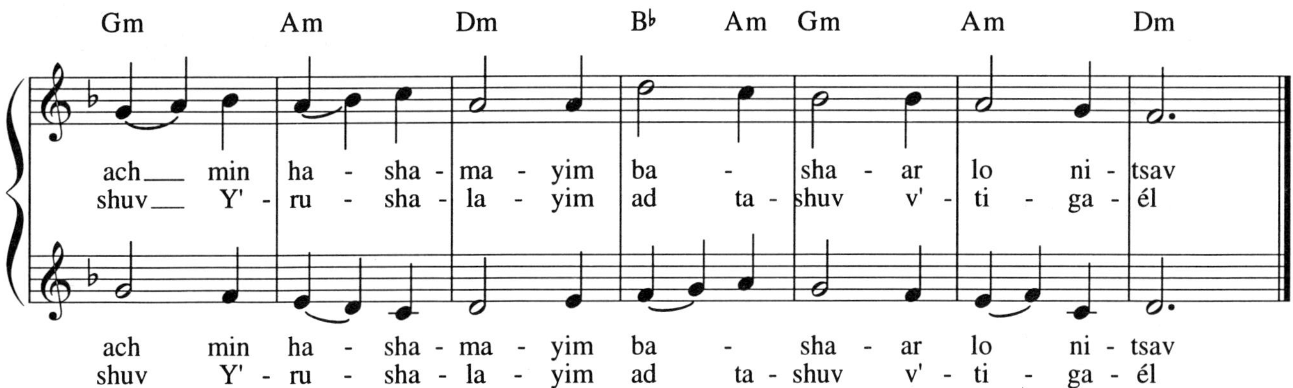

U-va-ir Y'-ru-sha-la-yim yésh sha-ar shel za-hav
U-mal-ach min ha-sha-ma-yim ba-sha-ar lo ni-tsav

Al mish-mar-to ze al-pa-yim hu ni-tsav yom va-lél
Ad ta-shuv Y'-ru-sha-la-yim ad ta-shuv v'-ti-ga-él

וּבָעִיר יְרוּשָׁלַיִם יֵשׁ שַׁעַר שֶׁל זָהָב
וּמַלְאָךְ מִן הַשָּׁמַיִם בַּשַּׁעַר לוֹ נִצָּב

עַל מִשְׁמַרְתּוֹ זֶה אַלְפַּיִם הוּא נִצָּב יוֹם וָלֵיל
עַד תָּשׁוּב יְרוּשָׁלַיִם עַד תָּשׁוּב וְתִגָּאֵל

In the city of Jerusalem stands a golden gate guarded by an angel. Thus has he stood day and night for two thousand years. Thus shall he stand until the city is once again ours.

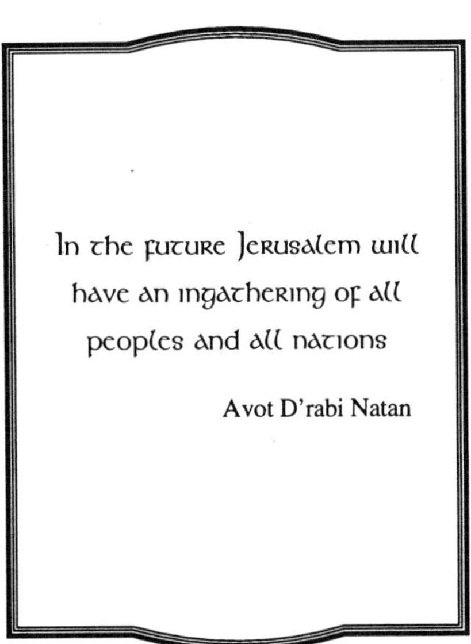

In the future Jerusalem will have an ingathering of all peoples and all nations

Avot D'rabi Natan

Sha'alu Shlom Y'rushalayim

Melody: Z. Borodi
Lyrics: Psalms
Arr: C. Goldberg

Allegro moderato

Am Em Am

Sha - a - lu sha - a - lu shlom Y' - ru - sha - la - yim ha - l' - lu ha - l' - lu - ya

Sha - a - lu sha - a - lu shlom Y' - ru - sha - la - yim ha - l' - lu ha - l' -

Sha - a - lu sha'a - lu ha -

E7 Am Em

sha - a - lu sha - a - lu shlom Y' - ru - sha - la - yim

lu - ya sha - a - lu sha - lom

ha - l' - lu - ha - l' - lu sha - a - lu sha - lom

Am Dm Esus4 E7 Am

ha - l' - lu ha - l' - lu - ya om - dot ha - yu

ha - l' - lu ha - l' - lu ha - l' - lu - ya om - dot ha -

ha - l' - ha - l' - lu - ya om - dot

C Dm G C

rag - lé - nu bish - a - ra - yich Y' - ru - sha - la - yim om -

yu rag - lé - nu Y' - ru - sha - la - yim om -

ha - yu bish - a - ra - yich Y' - ru - sha - la - yim

F C Dm

dot ha - yu rag - lé - nu bish - a - ra - yich Y' - ru - sha -

dot ha - yu rag - lé - nu Y' - ru - sha - la -

om - dot ha - yu rag - lé - nu bi - sh' - a - ra - yich Y' - ru - sha -

E Am Em

la - yim sha - a - lu sha - a - lu shlom Y' - ru - sha - la - yim

yim sha - a - lu sha - a - lu shlom Y' - ru - sha - la - yim

la - yim sha - a - lu sha'a - lu

Am E7 Am

ha - l' - lu ha - l' - lu - ya sha - a - lu sha - a - lu

ha - l' - lu ha - l' - lu - ya sha - a -

ha - l' - ha - l' - lu ha - l' - lu sha - a -

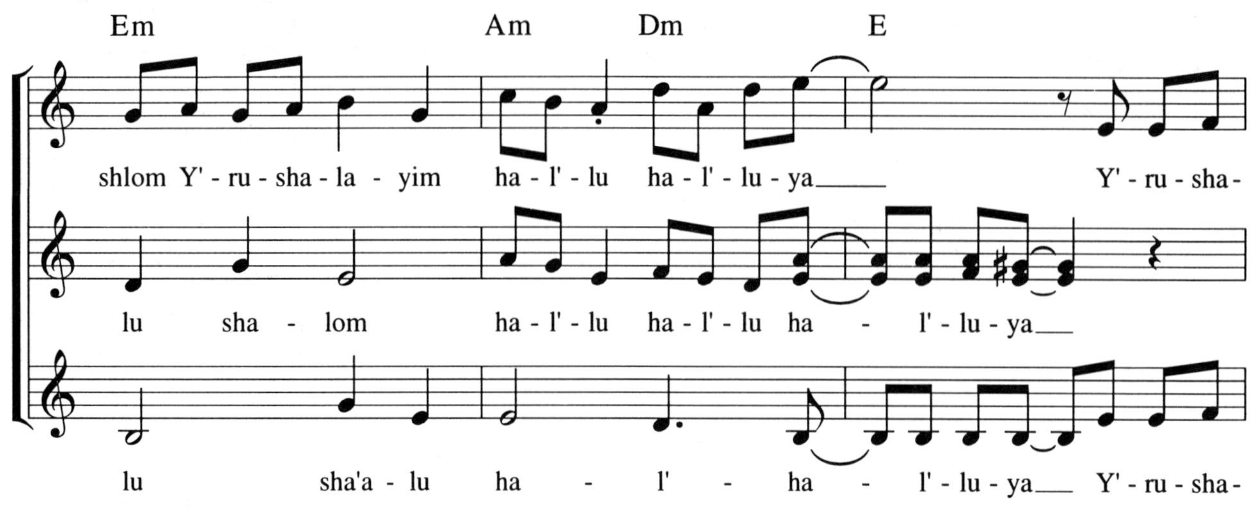

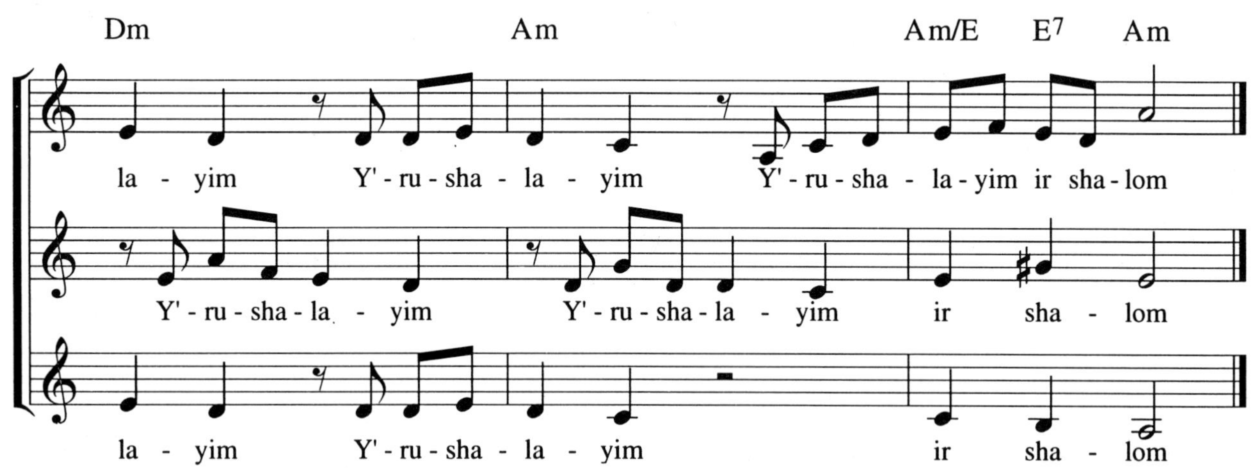

© by the author

Sha-a-lu sh'-lom Y'-ru-sha-la-yim	שַׁאֲלוּ שְׁלוֹם יְרוּשָׁלַיִם
Ha-l'-lu Ha-l'-lu-ya	הַלְלוּ הַלְלוּיָה
Om-dot ha-yu rag-lé-nu	עוֹמְדוֹת הָיוּ רַגְלֵינוּ
Bish-a-ra-yich Y'-ru-sha-la-yim	בִּשְׁעָרַיִךְ יְרוּשָׁלַיִם

Ask after the peace of Jerusalem. Ask, Haleluya. Our feet stood at your gates Jerusalem. Ask after the peace of Jerusalem. Ask, Haleluya. Jerusalem city of peace.

Music: D. Seltzer
Lyrics: J. Gamzu
Arr: S. Silbermintz

Slowly with feeling

Cm Fm Cm A♭6 Fm A♭
Am - da na - a - ra mul ha - ko - tel___ s'fa - ta - yim kér - va v' - san -

Cm B♭ E♭ Gm A♭ Fm
tér am - ra li t'ki - ot ha - sho - far cha - za - kot hén a -

Cm Fm G Cm Fm
val ha - sh'ti - ka od yo - tér am - ra li Tsi - yon har ha -

Cm A♭6 Fm A♭ Cm B♭ E♭ Gm
ba - yit___ shat - ka li ha - g'mul v' - ha - z'chut u - ma she - za - har al mits -

A♭7 Fm Cm A♭ G7
cha bén ar - ba - yim ha - ya ar - ga - man shel mal - chut

Cm A♭ Fm B♭ E♭ Cm7 E♭ Cm
Ha - ko - tel___ é - zov v' - a - tze - vet___ ha -

Ha - ko - tel é - zov v' - a - tse - vet___ ha -

Ha - ko - tel é - zov v' - a - tse - vet a - tse - vet ha -

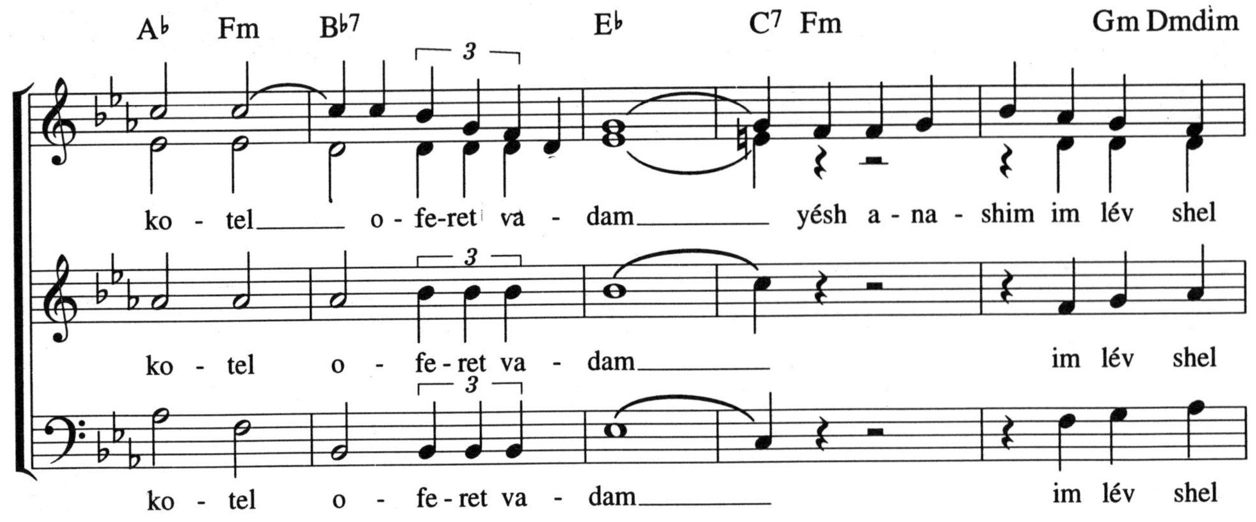

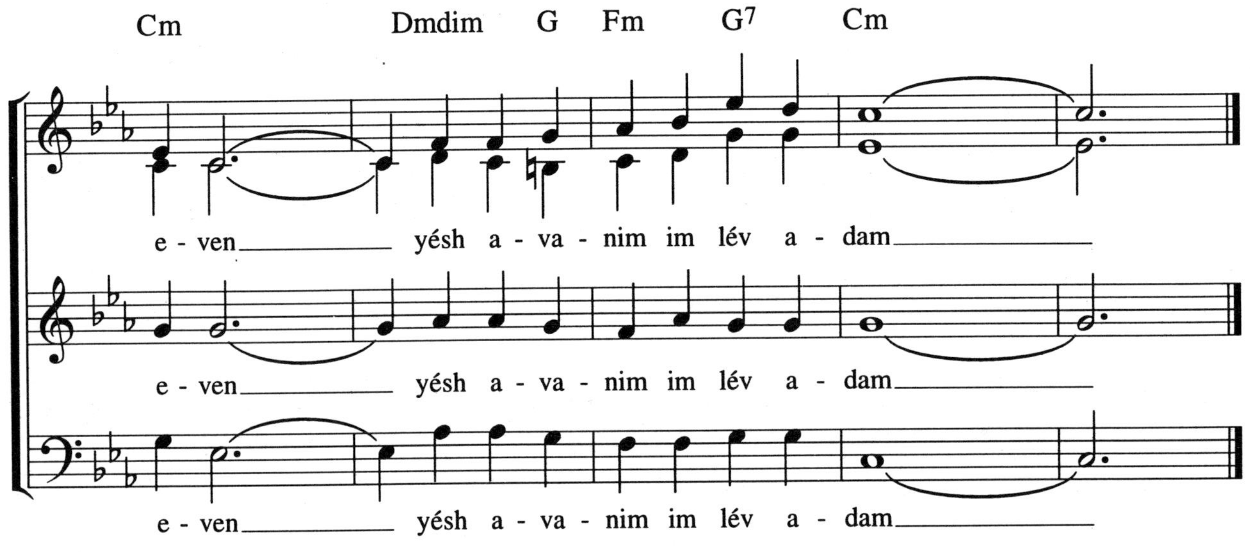

© by the authors

Am-da na-a-ra mul ha-ko-tel
S'-fa-ta-yim kér-va v'-san-tér
Am-ra li t'-ki-ot ha-sho-far cha-za-kot hén
A-val ha-sh'ti-ka od yo-tér
Am-ra li Tsi-yon har ha-ba-yit
Shat-ka li ha-g'-mul v'-ha-z'-chut
U-ma she-za-har al mits-cha bén ar-ba-yim
Ha-ya ar-ga-man shel mal-chut
Refrain
Ha-ko-tel é-zov v'-a-tse-vet
Ha-ko-tel o-fe-ret va-dam
Yésh a-na-shim im lév shel e-ven
Yésh a-va-nim im lév a-dam

עָמְדָה נַעֲרָה מוּל הַכֹּתֶל
שְׂפָתַיִם קָרְבָה וְסַנְטֵר
אָמְרָה לִי תְּקִיעוֹת הַשּׁוֹפָר חֲזָקוֹת הֵן
אֲבָל הַשְּׁתִיקָה עוֹד יוֹתֵר
אָמְרָה לִי צִיּוֹן הַר הַבַּיִת
שָׁתְקָה לִי הַגְּמוּל וְהַזְּכוּת
וּמַה שֶּׁזָּהַר עַל מִצְחָהּ בֵּין עַרְבַּיִם
הָיָה אַרְגָּמָן שֶׁל מַלְכוּת
פזמון
הַכֹּתֶל אֵזוֹב וְעַצֶּבֶת
הַכֹּתֶל עוֹפֶרֶת וָדָם
יֵשׁ אֲנָשִׁים עִם לֵב שֶׁל אֶבֶן
יֵשׁ אֲבָנִים עִם לֵב אָדָם

A-mad ha-tsan-chan mul ha-ko-tel
Mi-kol mach-lak-to rak e-chad
A-mar li "la-ma-vet én d'-mut ach yésh ko-ter
Tish-a mi-li-me-ter bil-vad"
A-mar li "é-ne-ni do-mé-a "
V'shav l'-hash-pil ma-ba-tim
Ach sa-ba she-li E-lo-him ha-yo-dé-a
Ka-vur kan b'-har ha-zé-tim Refrain

Am-da bish-cho-rim mul ha-ko-tel
I-mo shel e-chad min ha-chir
Am-ra li "é-né na-a-ri ha-dol-kot hén
V'-lo ha-né-rot she-ba-kir"
Am-ra li "é-ne-ni ro-she-met
Shum pe-tek lit-mon bén s'-da-kav
Ki ma she-na-ta-ti la-ko-tel rak e-mesh
Ga-dol mi-mi-lim u-mich-tav " Refrain

עָמַד הַצַנְחָן מוּל הַכֹּתֶל
מִכָּל מַחְלַקְתּוֹ רַק אֶחָד
אָמַר לִי לַמָּוֶת אֵין דְמוּת אַךְ יֵשׁ קֹטֶר
תִּשְׁעָה מִלְמֶטֶר בִּלְבַד
אָמַר לִי אֵינֶנִי דוֹמֵעַ
וְשָׁב לְהַשְׁפִּיל מַבָּטִים
אַךְ סַבָּא שֶׁלִי אֱלֹהִים הַיוֹדֵעַ
קָבוּר כָּאן בְּהַר הַזֵיתִים *פזמון*

עָמְדָה בִּשְׁחוֹרִים מוּל הַכֹּתֶל
אִמּוֹ שֶׁל אֶחָד מִן הַחִיי״ר
אָמְרָה לִי עֵינֵי נַעֲרִי הַדוֹלְקוֹת הֵן
וְלֹא הַנֵרוֹת שֶׁבַּקִיר
אָמְרָה לִי אֵינֶנִי רוֹשֶׁמֶת
שׁוּם פֶּתֶק לִטְמוֹן בֵּין סְדָקָיו
כִּי מַה שֶׁנָתַתִּי לַכֹּתֶל רַק אֶמֶשׁ
גָדוֹל מִמִלִים וּמִכְתָּב *פזמון*

A young girl, a paratrooper and a mother stand leaning against the Western Wall each deep in thought. There are men with hearts of stone; there are stones with hearts of men.

Vahavi'énu L'tsiyon

Music: Modzitz
Lyrics: Liturgy
Arr: V. Pasternak

Allegretto

Gm Cm Gm

Va - ha - vi - é - nu l' - tsi - yon ir - cha

Gm F B♭ Gm

l' - tsi - yon i - r' - cha b' - ri - na v' - li - ru - sha - la - yim

Cm Gm B♭ D7 1. Gm 2. Gm

bét mik - da - sh'- cha bét mik - da - sh' - cha b' - sim - chat o - lam lam

B♭ Cm B♭ Cm

va - ha - vi - é - nu l' - tsi - yon ir - cha l' - tsi - yon i - r' - cha

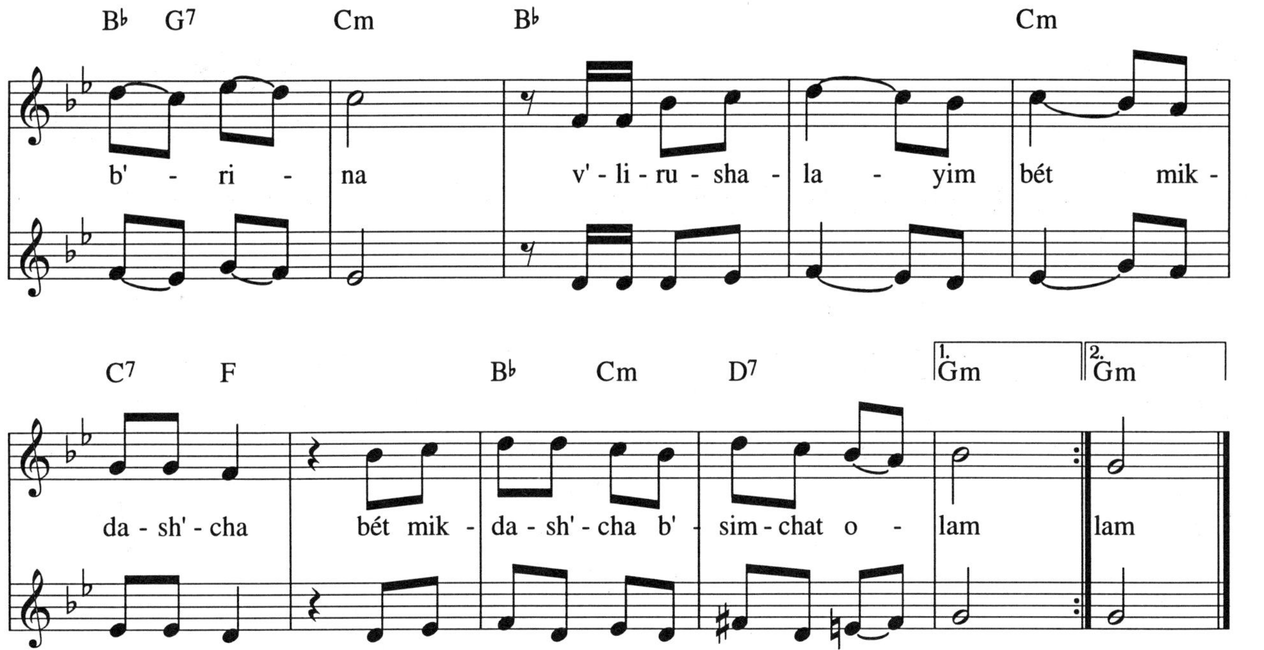

Va-ha-vi-é-nu l'-tsi-yon ir-cha b'-ri-na
V'-li-ru-sha-la-yim bét mik-dash-cha
B'-sim-chat o-lam

וַהֲבִיאֵנוּ לְצִיּוֹן עִירְךָ בְּרִנָּה
וְלִירוּשָׁלַיִם בֵּית מִקְדָּשְׁךָ
בְּשִׂמְחַת עוֹלָם

Lead us with exultation into Zion Your city, and into Jerusalem the place of Your sanctuary with everlasting joy.

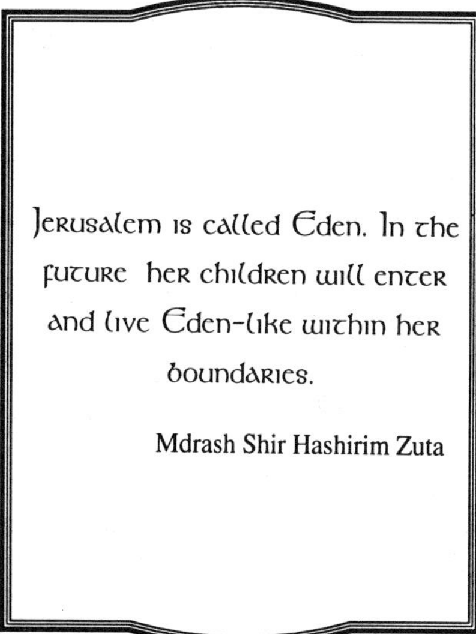

Omdot

Music: Melitzer Rebbe
Lyrics: Psalm 122
Arr: S. Silbermintz

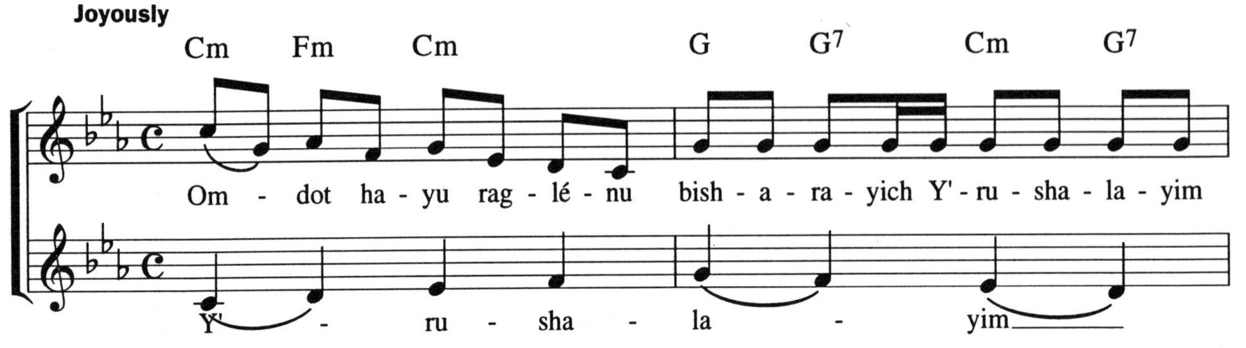

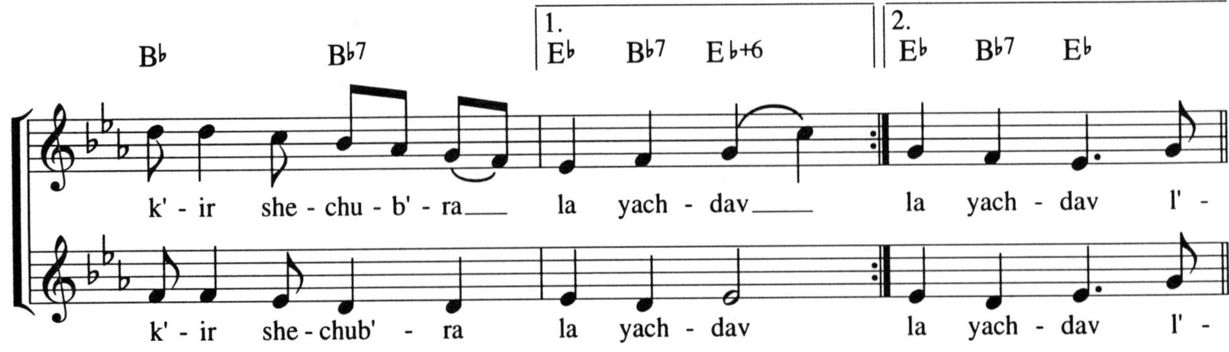

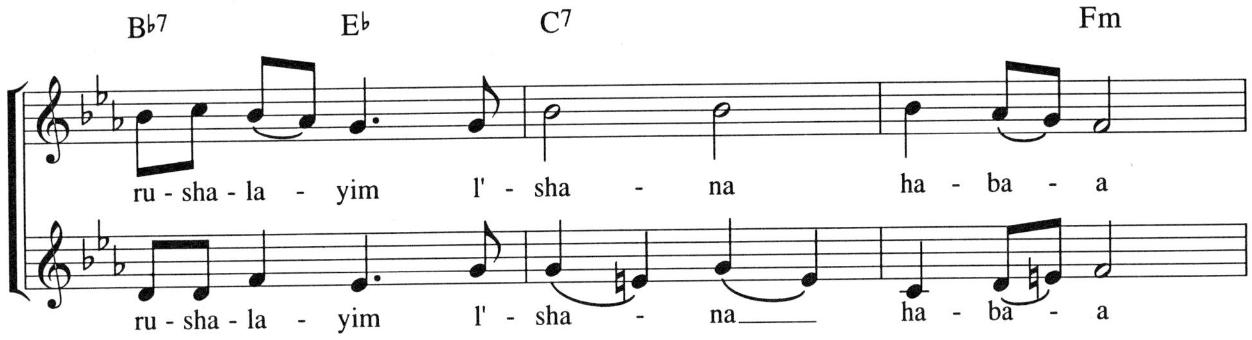

Om-dot ha-yu rag-lé-nu bish-a-ra-yich Y'-ru-sha-la-yim
Y'-ru-sha-la-yim ha-b'-nu-ya k'-ir she-chub-ra la yach-dav
L'- sha-na ha-ba-a bi-ru-sha-la-yim hab-nu-ya

עוֹמְדוֹת הָיוּ רַגְלֵינוּ בִּשְׁעָרַיִךְ יְרוּשָׁלָיִם
יְרוּשָׁלַיִם הַבְּנוּיָה כְּעִיר שֶׁחֻבְּרָה לָהּ יַחְדָּו
לַשָּׁנָה הַבָּאָה בִּירוּשָׁלַיִם הַבְּנוּיָה

Our feet stood within your gates. O Jerusalem—Jerusalem that is rebuilt like a city that is unified. Next year in Jerusalem!

Sheyibane Bét Hamikdash II

Music: M. Giladi
Lyrics: Liturgy
Arr: V. Pasternak

Moderately

G

3

She - yi - ba - ne bét ha - mik - dash she - yi - ba - ne she - yi - ba -

3

She - yi - ba - ne bét ha - mik - dash she - yi - ba - ne she - yi - ba -

G Em E7 Am

3

ne bét ha - mik - dash she - yi - ba - ne bim - hé -

ne bét ha - mik - dash she - yi - ba - ne bim - hé -

Am D7 G B Em

ra v' - ya - mé - nu she - yi - ba - ne bim - hé - ra v' - ya - mé - nu she - yi - ba - ne she -

ra v' - ya - mé - nu she - yi - ba - ne bim - hé - ra v' - ya - mé - nu she - yi - ba - ne she -

G D 1. G Am B7 2. G C G D E♭

yi - ba - ne bét ha - mik - dash bim - hé - dash she - yi - ba - ne she - yi - ba -

yi - ba - ne bét ha - mik - dash bim - hé - dash she - yi - ba - ne

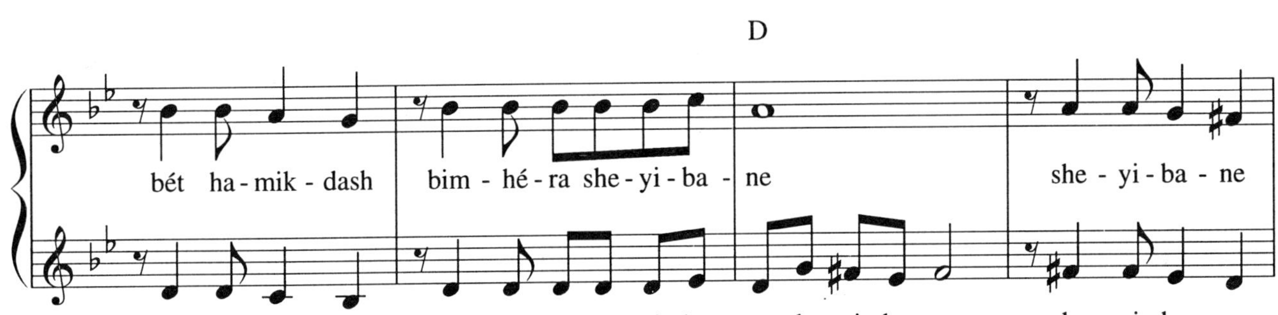

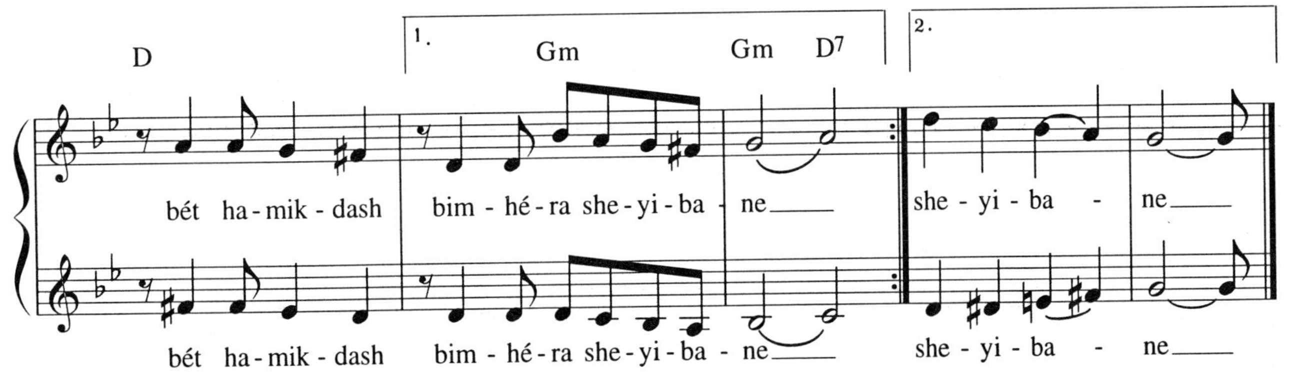

© by the author

She-yi-ba-ne bét ha-mik-dash
Bim-hé-ra v'-ya-mé-nu

שֶׁיִּבָּנֶה בֵּית הַמִּקְדָּשׁ
בִּמְהֵרָה בְיָמֵינוּ

May the Temple be speedily rebuilt in our days,
and grant us a share in Your Torah.

B'né Vétcha

Music: Modzitz
Lyrics: Liturgy
Arr: V. Pasternak

Moderately

Gm | Cm

B'- | né___ vét - cha b'- | né___ vét - cha b'-

1. Cm D7 Gm | 2. Cm D7 Gm

né___ vét - cha | vét - cha k'- vat - chi - la b'- | vét - cha k'- vat - chi - la v'-

F | B♭ Cm

cho - nén mik - dash - cha v'- | cho - nén mik - dash - cha v'- | cho - nén mik - dash - cha

1. B♭ Gm | 2. D D7 Gm

al___ m'- cho - no v'- | al m'- cho - no

© by the author

B'-né vét-cha k'-vat-chi-la
V'-cho-nén mik-dash-cha al m'-chono

בְּנֵה בֵיתְךָ כְּבַתְּחִלָּה
וְכוֹנֵן מִקְדָּשְׁךָ עַל מְכוֹנוֹ

Rebuild the Temple as of yore. Grant that we may see it rebuilt on its ancient site.

B'né Vétcha II

Music: I. Fuchs
Lyrics: Three Festivals Liturgy
Arr: S. Silbermintz

Spirited

Moderato [A]

Fm

Melody

B' - né vét - cha k' - vat - chi - la k' - vat - chi - la v' -

B' - né vét - cha k' - vat - chi - la k' - vat - chi - la v' -

Fm [B] Fm B♭m6/4

cho - nén mik - dash - cha___ al m' - cho - no b' - vin -

al___ m' - cho - no v' - har - é - nu b' - vin - ya - no

Melody

cho - nén mik - dash - cha___ al m' - cho - no b' - vin -

Fm Fm E♭ E♭7 A♭

ya - no v' - sam - ché - nu v' - sam - ché - nu b' - ti - ku - no

melody

v' - sam - ché - nu b' - ti - ku - no v' - sam - ché - nu b' - ti - ku - no

ya - no v' - sam - ché - nu v' - sam - ché - nu b' - ti - ku - no

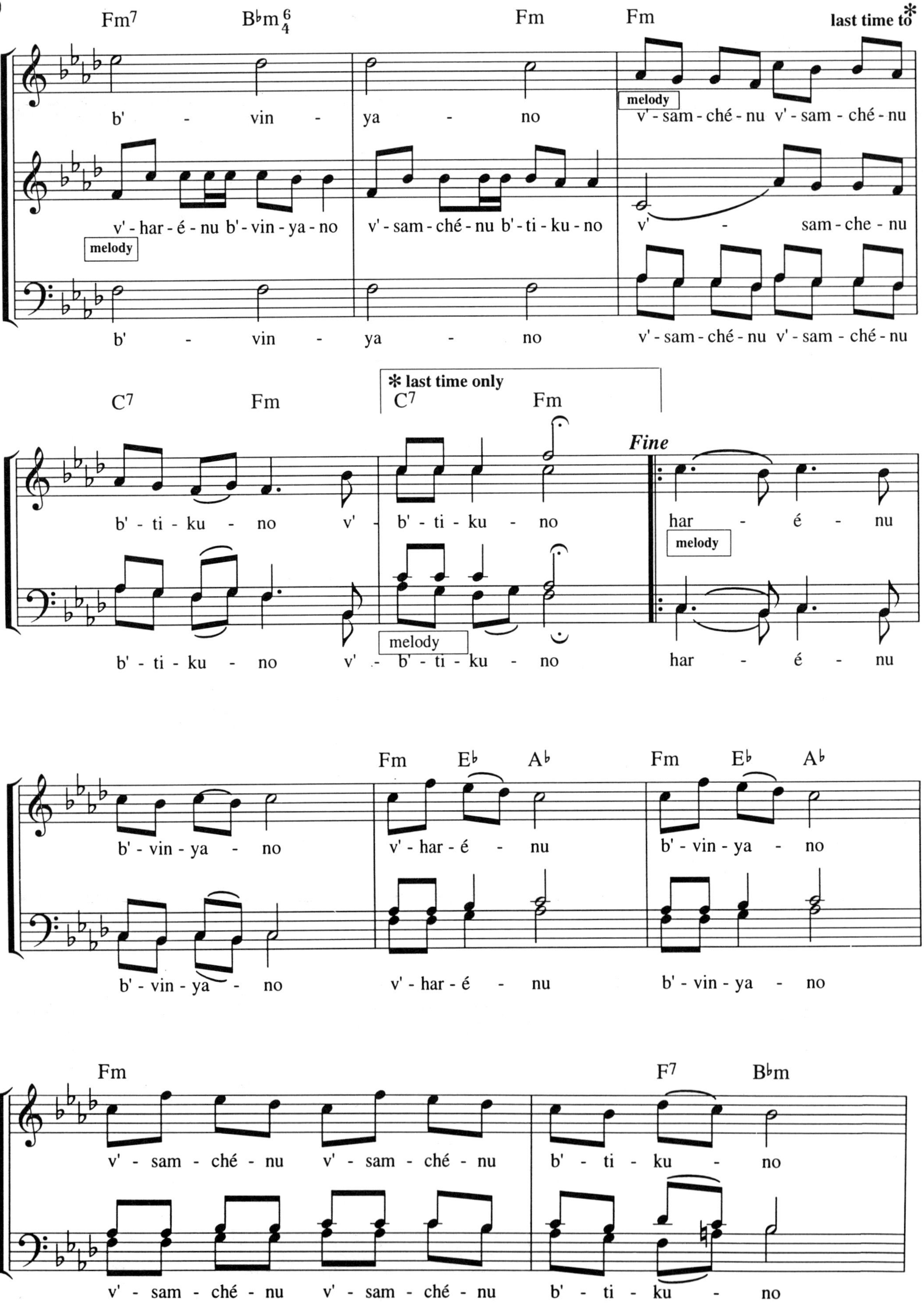

Fm7 B♭m 6/4 Fm Fm last time to*

b' - vin - ya - no v' - sam - ché - nu v' - sam - ché - nu

melody

v' - har - é - nu b' - vin - ya - no v' - sam - ché - nu b' - ti - ku - no v' - sam - che - nu

melody

b' - vin - ya - no v' - sam - ché - nu v' - sam - ché - nu

C7 Fm *last time only C7 Fm *Fine*

b' - ti - ku - no v' - b' - ti - ku - no har - é - nu

melody

melody

b' - ti - ku - no v' - b' - ti - ku - no har - é - nu

Fm E♭ A♭ Fm E♭ A♭

b' - vin - ya - no v' - har - é - nu b' - vin - ya - no

b' - vin - ya - no v' - har - é - nu b' - vin - ya - no

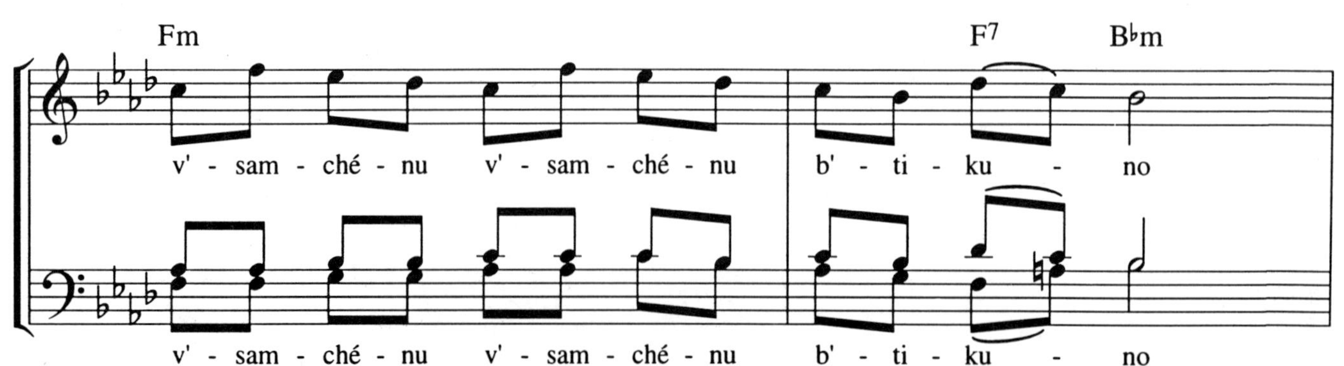

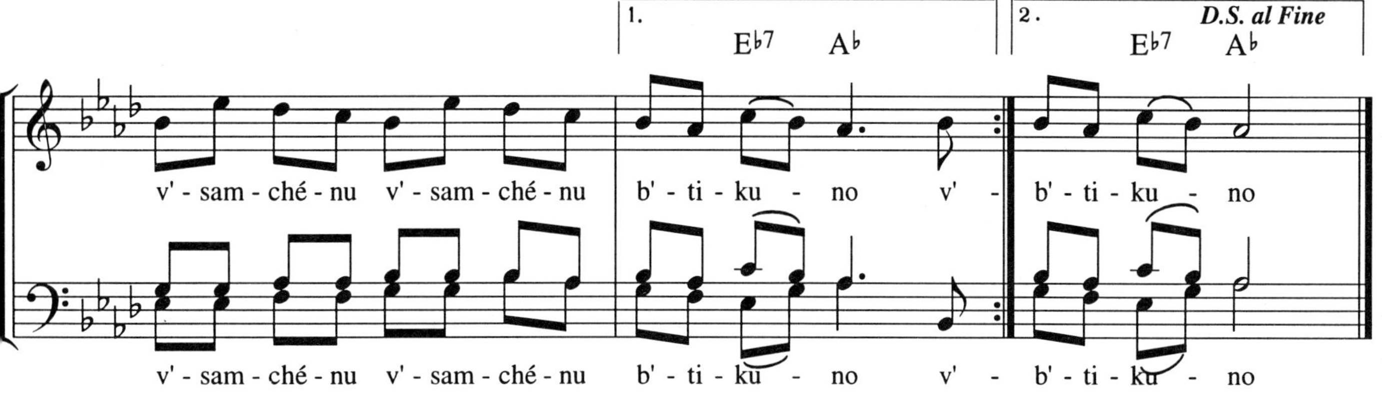

© by the author

B'-né vét-cha k'-vat-chi-la
V'-cho-nén mik-dash-cha al m'-chono
V'-har-é-nu b'-vin-ya-no v'-sam-ché-nu b'-ti-ku-no

בְּנֵה בֵיתְךָ כְּבַתְּחִלָּה
וְכוֹנֵן מִקְדָּשְׁךָ עַל מְכוֹנוֹ
וְהַרְאֵנוּ בְּבִנְיָנוֹ וְשַׂמְּחֵנוּ בְּתִקּוּנוֹ

Rebuild the Temple as of yore. Grant that we may see it rebuilt on its ancient site.

M'héra Yishama

Music: Modzitz
Lyrics: Wedding Liturgy
Arr: V. Pasternak

Vivace

M'- hé - ra yi - sha - ma b' - a - ré Y' - hu - da u - v' - chu - tsot Y' - ru - sha - la - yim

kol sa - son v' - kol sim - cha kol chan - tan v' - kol ka - la

kol mits - ha - lot cha - ta - nim mé - chu - pa - tam u - n' - a - rim mi - mish - té n' - gi - na - tam gi - na - tam

M'-hé-ra yi-sha-ma b'-a-ré Y'-hu-da
Uv'-chu-tsot Y'-ru-sha-la-yim
Kol sa-son v'-kol sim-cha
Kol cha-tan v'-kol ka-la
Kol mits-ha-lot cha-ta-nim mé-chu-pa-tam
U-n'-a-rim mi-mish-te n'-gi-na-tam

מְהֵרָה יִשָּׁמַע בְּעָרֵי יְהוּדָה
וּבְחוּצוֹת יְרוּשָׁלַיִם
קוֹל שָׂשׂוֹן וְקוֹל שִׂמְחָה
קוֹל חָתָן וְקוֹל כַּלָּה
קוֹל מִצְהֲלוֹת חֲתָנִים מֵחֻפָּתָם
וּנְעָרִים מִמִּשְׁתֵּה נְגִינָתָם

Soon may there be heard in the cities of Judah and in the streets of Jerusalem, the voice of joy and gladness, the voice of bridegroom and bride, the jubilant voice of bridegrooms from their canopies, and of youths from their feasts of song.

Uri Tsiyon

Music: M. Wilensky
Lyrics: Isaiah 52:1
Arr: S. Silbermintz

Allegro moderato

E♭ A♭ E♭

U - ri Tsi - yon Tsi - yon u - ri___

𝄋 E♭ E♭ Fm E♭ Fm 1. E♭

U - ri Tsi - yon hoy u - ri liv - shi u - zéch u - ri Tsi - yon hoy u - ri___

U - ri Ts - yon Tsi - yon u - ri___

2. E♭ ⊕ B♭ B♭m Fm E♭ Fm

u - ri___ liv - shi big - dé tif - ar - téch Y' - ru - sha - la - yim ir ha - ko -
ki lo yo - sif ya - vo vach lo yo - sif ya - vo vach od a - rél___ v' - ta -

u - ri___ Y' - ru - sha - la - yim ir ha -
lo ya - vo vach___ v' - ta -

B♭sus B♭ B♭m Fm E♭ Fm

desh___ liv - shi big - dé tif - ar - téch Y' - ru - sha - la - yim Y' - ru - sha - la - yim
mé___ ki lo yo - sif ya - vo vach lo yo - sif ya - vo vach od___ a - rél___

ko - desh Y' - ru - sha - la - yim Y' - ru - sha - la - yim
mé___ lo ya - vo vach___ od a - rél___

B♭ Cm7-5 C♯dim B♭7 E♭ Fm E♭ Fm
ir ha - ko - desh u - ri Tsi - yon hoy u - ri liv - shi u - zéch u - ri Tsi - yon hoy
v' - ta - mé hey!
ir ha - ko - desh u - ri Tsi - yon Tsi - yon
v' - ta - mé hey!
1. E♭ 2. E♭ Fm Cm
u - ri u - ri hit - na - a - ri mé - a - far mé - a -
melody
u - ri u - ri hit - na - a - ri hit - na - a - ri mé - a - far hit - na - a -
Fm B♭ Cm Fm Cm
far ku - mi hit - na - a - ri mé - a - far Y' -
ri mé - a - far ku - mi hit - na - a - ri hit - na - a - ri mé - a - far hit - na - a -
CODA
Fm B♭7 Gmsus Gm Gm Cm7 B♭
D.S. al e poi al Coda
ru - sha - la - yim u - ri u - ri u - ri
ri Y' - ru - sha - la - yim u - ri u - ri u - ri
E♭ Fm7 B♭7 E♭ Gm E♭ D♭ E♭
rit.
u - ri Tsi - yon hoy u - ri u - ri Tsi - yon
u - ri Tsi - yon hoy u - ri u - ri Tsi - yon

עוּרִי צִיּוֹן הוֹי עוּרִי לִבְשִׁי עֻזֵּךְ
לִבְשִׁי בִּגְדֵי תִּפְאַרְתֵּךְ יְרוּשָׁלַיִם עִיר הַקֹּדֶשׁ
כִּי לֹא יוֹסִיף יָבֹא בָךְ עוֹד עָרֵל וְטָמֵא הֵא!
הִתְנַעֲרִי מֵעָפָר הִתְנַעֲרִי יְרוּשָׁלַיִם

U-ri Tsi-yon hoy u-ri liv-shi u-zéch
Liv-shi big-dé tif-ar-téch Y'-ru-sha-la-yim ir ha-ko-desh
Ki lo yo-sif ya-vo vach od a-rél v'-ta-mé hey!
Hit-na-a-ri mé-a-far hit-na-a-ri Y'-ru-sha-la-yim

©Tarbut Vechinuch Ed.

Awake, O Zion, and put on your strength. Put on your beautiful garments, O Jerusalem, the holy city; for henceforth the unclean shall come no more into you. Shake yourself from the dust. Arise, Jerusalem.

Tén Shabat

Music: D. Seltzer
Lyrics: C. Hefer
Arr: S. Gewirtz

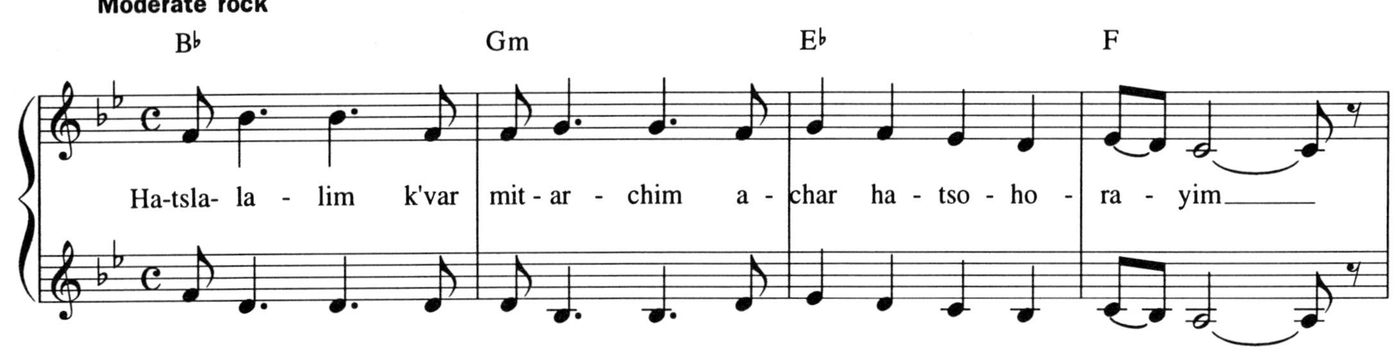

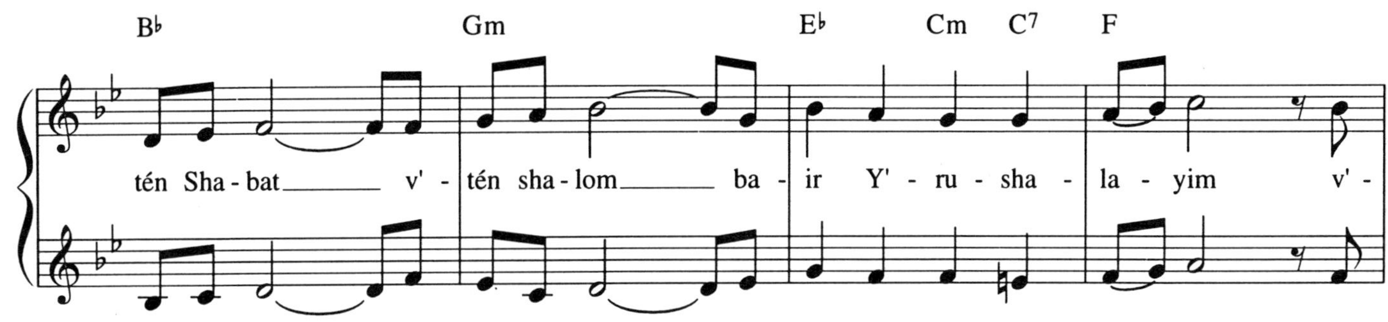

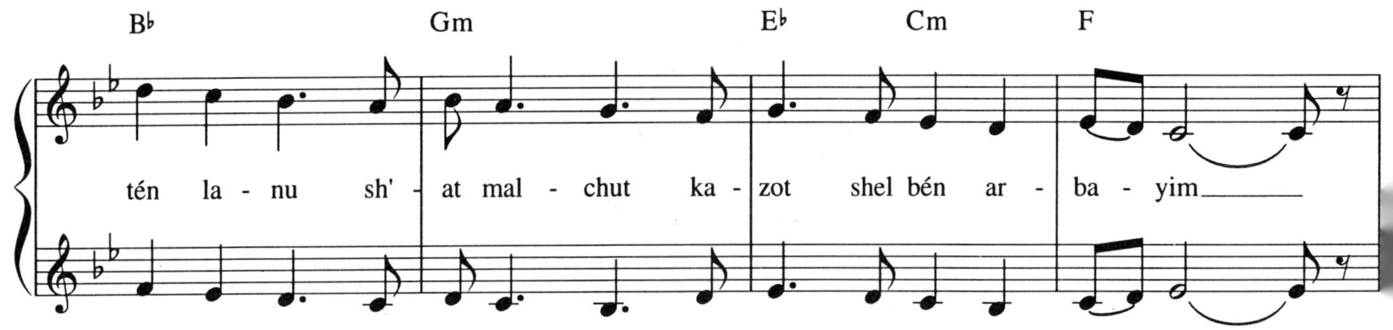

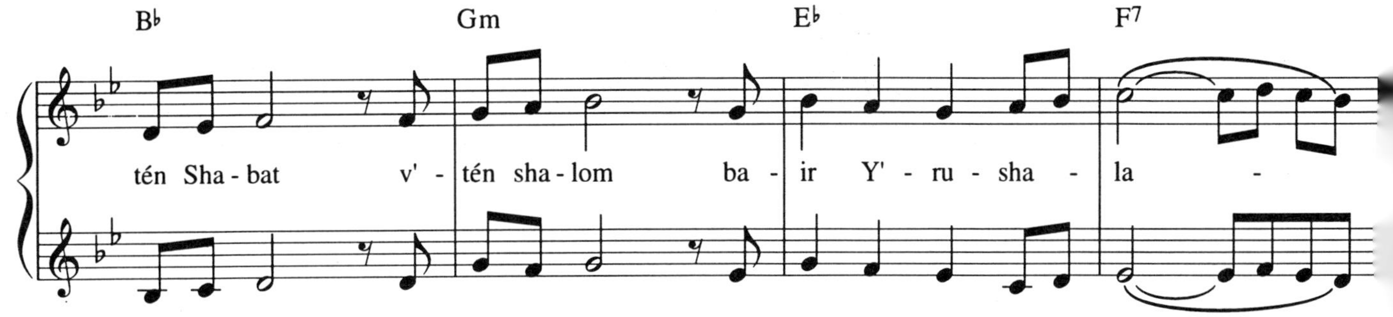

©by the authors

Hats-la-lim k'var mit-ar-chim
A-char ha-tso-ho-ra-yim
Tén Sha-bat v'-tén sha-lom ba-ir Y'-ru-sha-la-yim
V'-tén la-nu sh'-at mal-chut ka-zot shel bén ar-ba-yim
Tén Sha-lom v'-tén Sha-bat ba-ir Y'-ru-sha-la-yim

הַצְּלָלִים כְּבָר מִתְאָרְכִים
אַחַר הַצָּהֳרַיִם
תֵּן שַׁבָּת וְתֵן שָׁלוֹם בָּעִיר יְרוּשָׁלַיִם
וְתֵן לָנוּ שְׁעַת מַלְכוּת כָּזֹאת שֶׁל בֵּין עַרְבָּעִים
תֵּן שָׁלוֹם וְתֵן שַׁבָּת בָּעִיר יְרוּשָׁלַיִם

Refrain
Tén Sha-bat v'-tén sha-lom
Ba-ir Y'-ru-sha-la-yim

פזמון
תֵּן שַׁבָּת וְתֵן שָׁלוֹם
בָּעִיר יְרוּשָׁלַיִם

Hi-né ba-a ha-sha-bat im so-mek ha-sha-ma-yim
Tén Sha-bat v'-tén sha-lom ba-ir Y'-ru-sha-la-yim
Hi-né sha-lom yo-réd a-lai yo-réd bits-ror ch'-na-fa-yim
Tén sha-lom v'-tén Sha-bat ba-ir Y'-ru-sha-la-yim Refrain

הִנֵּה בָּאָה הַשַּׁבָּת עִם סוֹמֶק הַשָּׁמַיִם
תֵּן שַׁבָּת וְתֵן שָׁלוֹם בָּעִיר יְרוּשָׁלַיִם
הִנֵּה שָׁלוֹם יוֹרֵד עָלַי יוֹרֵד בִּצְרוֹר כְּנָפַיִם
תֵּן שָׁלוֹם וְתֵן שַׁבָּת בָּעִיר יְרוּשָׁלַיִם *פזמון*

Kol ha-mig-da-lim ku-lam mish-ta-cha-vim a-pa-yim
Tén Sha-bat v'-tén sha-lom ba-ir Y'-ru-sha-la-yim
Or ga-dol hi-né nid-lak b'-i-sho-né é-na-yim
Tén sha-lom v'-tén Sha-bat ba-ir Y'-ru-sha-la-yim Refrain

כָּל הַמִּגְדָּלִים כֻּלָּם מִשְׁתַּחֲוִים אַפַּיִים
תֵּן שַׁבָּת וְתֵן שָׁלוֹם בָּעִיר יְרוּשָׁלַיִם
אוֹר גָּדוֹל הִנֵּה נִדְלַק בְּאִשׁוֹנֵי עֵינַיִם
תֵּן שָׁלוֹם וְתֵן שַׁבָּת בָּעִיר יְרוּשָׁלַיִם

The afternoon shadows have grown longer. Behold peace descends on the approaching Sabbath. Grant Sabbath rest and peace in Jerusalem.

Hal'lu Lirushalayim II

Music: Aharony
Lyrics: Traditional

Allegro moderato

F

Ha - l' - lu ha - l' - lu na | ha - l' - lu li - ru - sha - la - yim | ha - l' - lu ha - l' - lu na

Ha - l' - lu ha - l' - lu na | ha - l' - lu ha - l' - lu | ha - l' - lu ha - l' - lu na

1. C11 2. C Bb F

l' - tsi - yon | l' - tsi - yon | ha - l' - lu na | li - ru - sha - la - yim

l' - tsi - yon | l' - tsi - yon | ha - l' - lu na | li - ru - sha - la - yim

Ha-l'-lu li-ru-sha-la-yim
Ha-l'-lu na l'-tsi-yon

הַלְלוּ נָא לִירוּשָׁלַיִם
הַלְלוּ נָא לְצִיּוֹן

Praise Jerusalem and Zion.

f I Forget Thee O Jerusalem

usic: I. Antelis
yrics: D. Grossman

Andante con espressivo

Fm Cm D♭ A♭/C

Loo loo loo loo loo loo loo loo loo loo loo loo loo loo loo loo loo

loo loo loo loo loo

C
B♭m Fm Cm D♭ A♭/C

loo loo If I for - get thee O Je - ru - sa - lem should I lose the will — to —

loo loo If I for - get thee O Je - ru - sa - lem should I lose the will — to —

B♭m C7 Fm Cm D♭m E♭/D♭ Cm Fm

hope If I could ne - ver see your gold - en hill my right hand pow-er-less and

hope If I could ne - ver see your gold - en hill my right hand pow- er- less and

B♭m7 C7 Fm Cm D♭

still ——— If I for - get thee O Je - ru - sa - lem (1) Think-ing (2) From my

still ——— If I for - get ——— If I for - get

A♭/C B♭m C7 Fm Cm
on - ly of this new — land not speak-ing lov - ing - ly of our home -
birth un - til — my — death ne - ver to taste the milk of your sweet
If I for - get Je - ru - sa - lem our — home
your — sweet
D♭m E♭/D♭ Cm7 Fm7 B♭m7 C7
land speak in tongues none could un - der - stand With a
land ne - ver lie deep be- neath your sand
land speak — in — tongues — none could un - der - stand With a
land ne - ver — lie — deep be - neath your sand —
F B♭m E♭
dream of a new to - mor - row with a dream of a hea - ven on
With a dream — of a new to - mor-row with a dream —
A♭ D♭ B♭7/D A♭/E♭ Fm
earth Vis- ions of po - ets and pro - phets that burn in our soul —
— of a hea- ven on earth — po - ets, proph- ets that burn in our soul —
B♭m7 E♭ C7 F
since our peo - ple's birth With a dream of a new to -
since our peo - ple's birth — With a with a dream —

B♭m E♭ 3 A♭
mor - row with a dream of a hea - ven on earth we shall re -
of a new to - mor - row with a dream of a hea - ven on earth
D♭ 3 B♭7/D 3 A♭/E♭ 3 Fm 1. B♭m7 E♭
turn to our home to the wall made of stone once a - gain re - birth If I for -
to our home to the wall made of stone once a - gain re - birth If I for -
2. B♭m7 E♭ Fm A7/G D D7
Once a - gain re - birth If I for - get thee O Je - ru - sa - lem with a
If I for - get Je - ru - sa - lem with a
G Cm F 3
dream of a new to - mor - row with a dream of a hea - ven on
with a dream of a new to - mor - row with a dream
B♭ E♭ 3 C7/E 3 B♭/F 3 Gm
earth vis - ions of po - ets and proph - ets that burn in our soul
of a hea - ven on earth po - ets, proph - ets that burn in our soul

©by the authors

If I forget thee O Jerusalem
Should I lose the will to hope
If I could never see your golden hills
My right hand powerless and still

If I forget thee O Jerusalem
Thinking only of this new land
Not speaking lovingly of our homeland
Speak in tongues none could understand.

With a dream of a new tomorrow
With a dream of a heaven and earth
Visions of poets and prophets
That burn in our soul
Since our people's birth.

With a dream of a new tomorrow
With a dream of a heaven and earth
We shall return to our home
To the wall made of stone
Once again rebirth.
If I forget thee O Jerusalem
From my birth until my death
Never to taste the milk of your sweet land
Never lie deep beneath your sand

Y'rushalém Hi Keter Ha'olam

Music: H. Bratter
Lyrics: S. Or
Arr: C. Goldberg

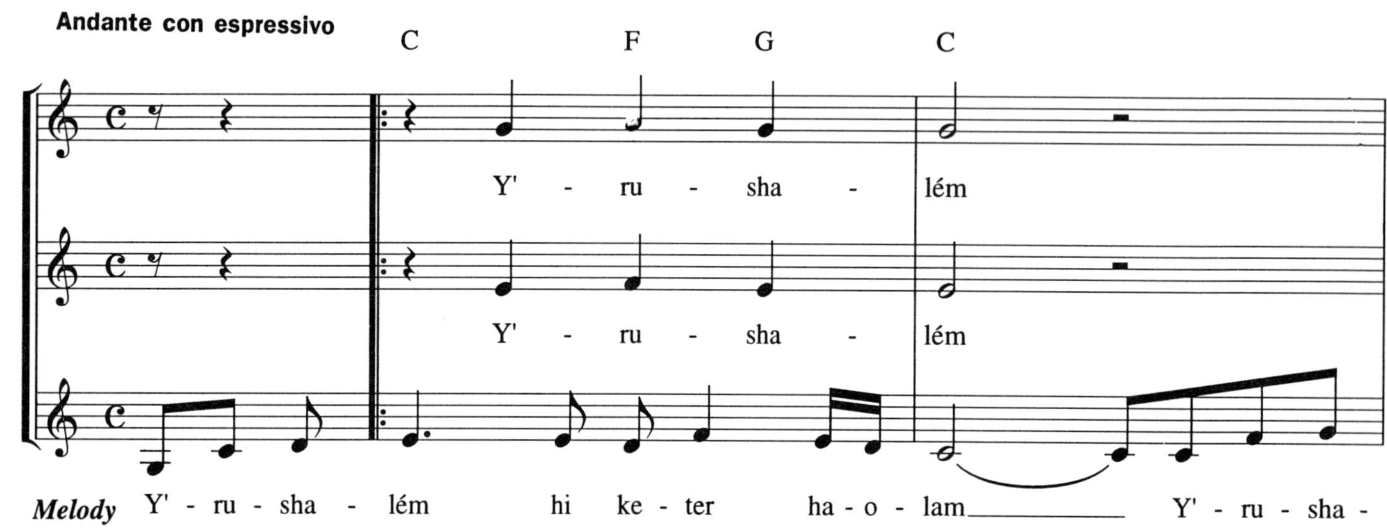

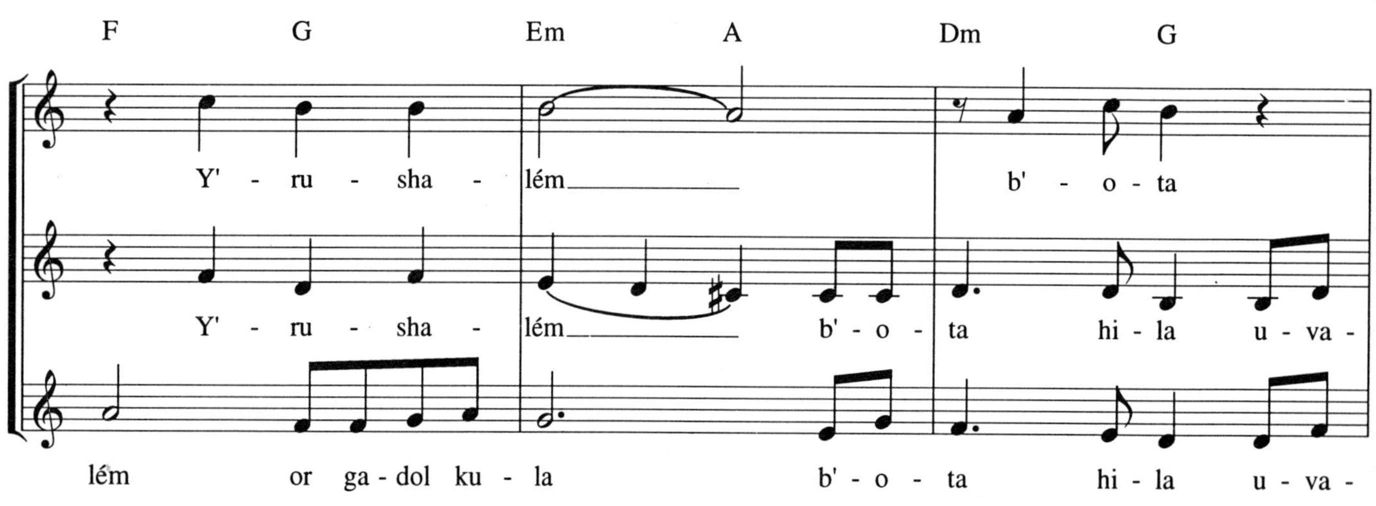

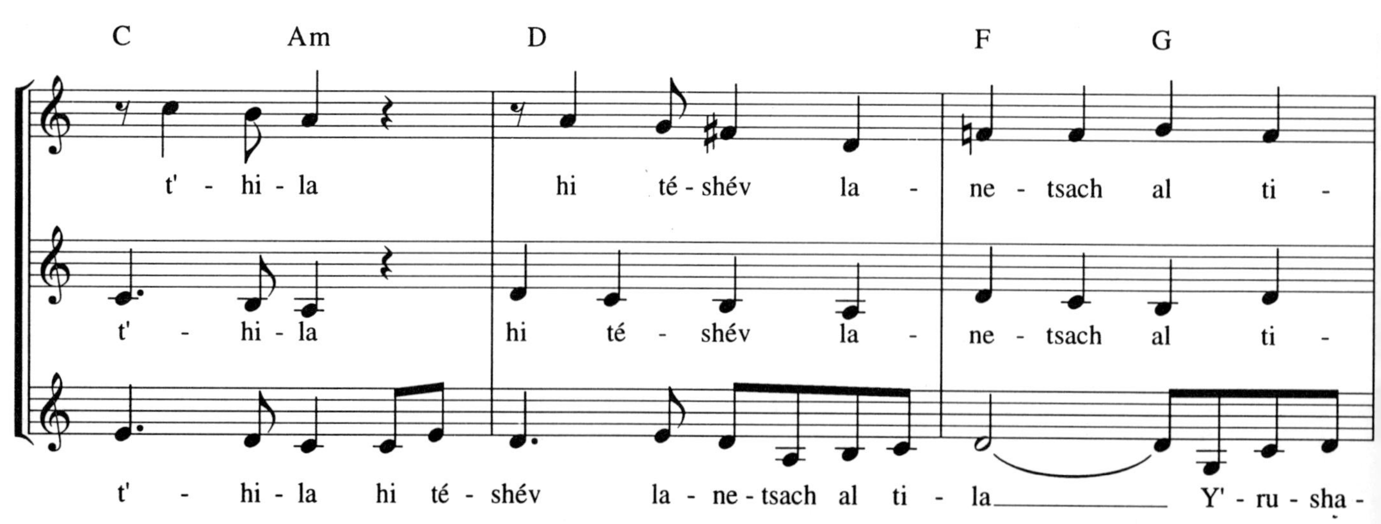

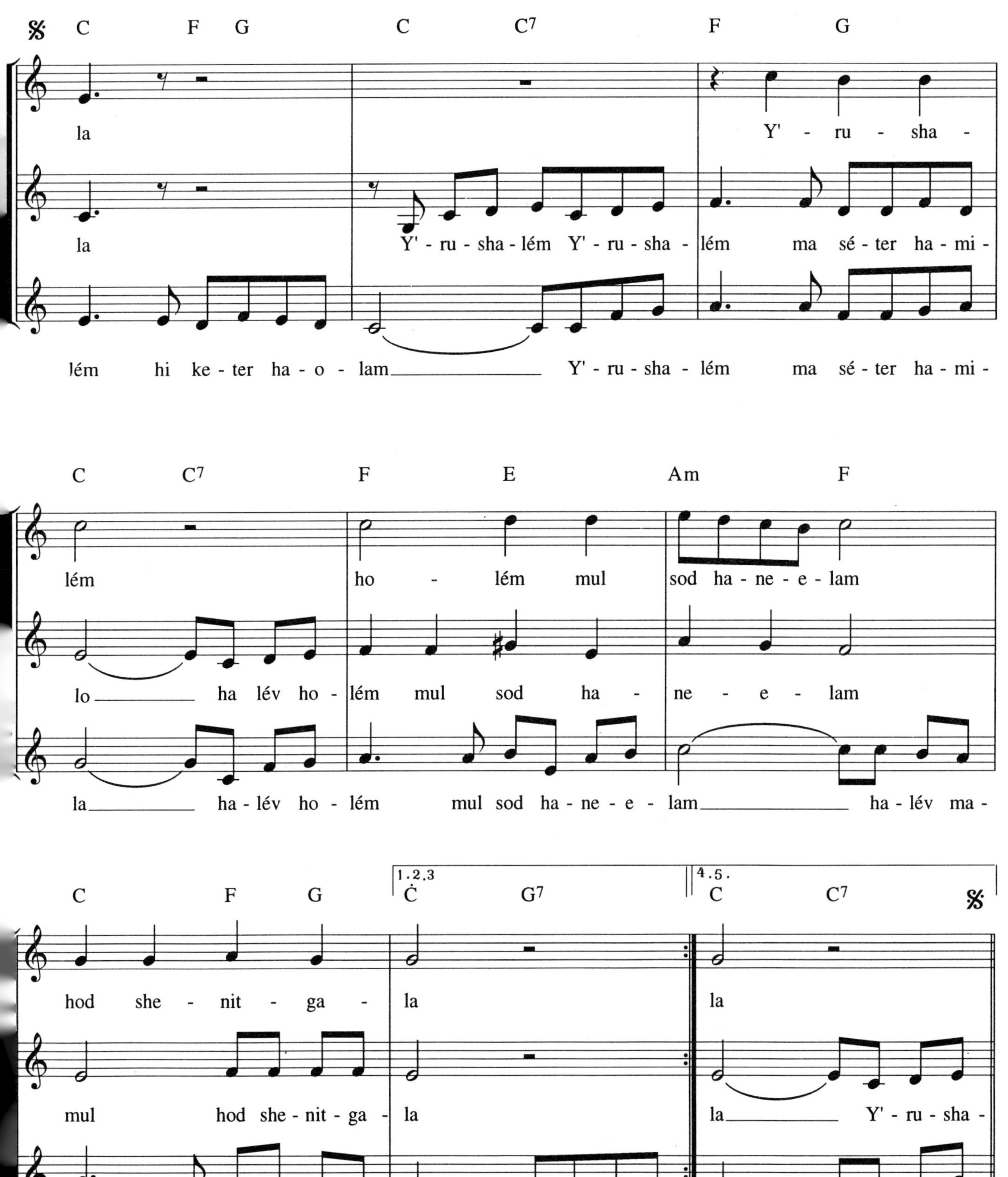
C F G C C7 F G
la
Y' - ru - sha -
la
Y' - ru - sha - lém Y' - ru - sha - lém ma sé - ter ha - mi -
lém hi ke - ter ha - o - lam Y' - ru - sha - lém ma sé - ter ha - mi -
C C7 F E Am F
lém ho - lém mul sod ha - ne - e - lam
lo ha lév ho - lém mul sod ha - ne - e - lam
la ha - lév ho - lém mul sod ha - ne - e - lam ha - lév ma -
1.2.3
4.5.
C F G C G7 C C7
hod she - nit - ga - la
la
mul hod she - nit - ga - la
la Y' - ru - sha -
le mul hod she - nit - ga - la Y' - ru - sha - la
la Y' - ru - sha -

F E F C F G
té - shév la - ne - tsach al ti - la Y' - ru - sha - lém Y' - ru - sha -
lém la - ne - tsach al ti - la Y' - ru - sha -
lém la - ne - tsach al ti la Y' - ru - sha -
F Dm G C
lém Y' - ru - sha - lém
lém Y' - ru - sha - lém
lém Y' - ru - sha - lém
©by the authors
ENTRANCE TO MEA SHEARIM

Y'-ru-sha-lém hi ke-ter ha-o-lam	יְרוּשָׁלֵם הִיא כֶּתֶר הָעוֹלָם
Y'-ru-sha-lém or ga-dol ku-la	יְרוּשָׁלֵם אוֹר גָדוֹל כֻּלָה
B'-o-ta hi-la u-vat-hi-la	בְּאוֹתָה הִלָה וּבַתְהִלָה
Hi té-shév la-ne-tsach al ti-la	הִיא תֵּשֵׁב לָנֶצַח עַל תִּלָה
Refrain	*פזמון*
Y'-ru-sha-lém hi ke-ter ha-o-lam	יְרוּשָׁלֵם הִיא כֶּתֶר הָעוֹלָם
Y'-ru-sha-lém ma sé-ter ha-mi-la	יְרוּשָׁלֵם מַה סֵתֶר הַמִלָה
Ha-lév ho-lém mul sod ha-ne-e-lam	הַלֵב הוֹלֵם מוּל סוֹד הַנֶעֱלַם
Ha-lév ma-lé mul hod she-nit-ga-la Refrain	הַלֵב מָלֵא מוּל הוֹד שֶׁנִתְגַלָה
Y'-ru-sha-lém hi sof v'-hat-cha-la	יְרוּשָׁלֵם הִיא סוֹף וְהַתְחָלָה
Y'-ru-sha-lém hi chof v'-na-cha-la	יְרוּשָׁלֵם הִיא חוֹף וְנַחֲלָה
Kol ish o-le é-le-ha vam-si-la	כָּל אִישׁ עוֹלֶה אֵלֶיהָ בַּמְסִילָה
Kol ish cho-lém é-le-ha ba-t'-fi-la Refrain	כָּל אִישׁ חוֹלֵם אֵלֶיהָ בַּתְּפִלָה *פזמון*
Y'-ru-sha-lém hi sof v'-hat-cha-la	יְרוּשָׁלֵם הִיא סוֹף וְהַתְחָלָה
Y'-ru-sha-lém hi chof v'-na-cha-la	יְרוּשָׁלֵם הִיא חוֹף וְנַחֲלָה
Hi-né sha-vim ba-de-rech ha-o-la	הִנֵה שָׁבִים בַּדֶרֶךְ הָעוֹלָה
Hi-né sha-vim ba-ne-ha lig-vu-la Refrain	הִנֵה שָׁבִים בָּנֶיהָ לִגְבוּלָה *פזמון*
Y'-ru-sha-la-yim hi-ke-ter ha-o-lam	יְרוּשָׁלֵם הִיא כֶּתֶר הָעוֹלָם
Y'-ru-sha-lém hi sof v'-hat-cha-la	יְרוּשָׁלֵם הִיא סוֹף וְהַתְחָלָה
Hi-né sha-vim ba-de-rech ha-o-la	הִנֵה שָׁבִים בַּדֶרֶךְ הָעוֹלָה
Hi-né sha-vim va-ne-ha lig-vu-la	הִנֵה שָׁבִים בָּנֶיהָ לִגְבוּלָה
Y'-ru-sha-lém la-ne-tsach al ti-la	יְרוּשָׁלֵם לָנֶצַח עַל תִּלָה
Y'-ru-sha-lém Y'-ru-sha-lém	יְרוּשָׁלֵם יְרוּשָׁלֵם

Jerusalem is the crown of the world. Jerusalem is filled with a great light. She will forever sit up high on her hill. What is the secret of the word "crown"? The heart beats to the hidden secret, the heart is filled with the majesty uncovered. Jerusalem is the beginning and the end, Jerusalem is the shore and the stream. All ascend to her, all dream of her in prayer.

Ki Mitsiyon III

Music: E. Amiran
Lyrics: Liturgy

Spirited

Gm Dm C E♭ Gm Dm Am Cm Gm F
Ki mi - tsi - yon hoy té - tsé To - ra ki mi -
Ki mi - tsi - yon hoy té - tsé To - ra ki mi -

C E♭ Cm F Gm B♭ Dm
tsi - yon hoy té - tsé To - ra u - d'var Ha - shem
tsi - yon hoy té - tsé To - ra u - d'var Ha - shem

Gm Am Gm C7 A7 Dm Gm A7 Dm
ud - var Ha - shem ud - var Ha - shem mi - ru - sha - la - yim
ud - var Ha - shem ud - var Ha - shem mi - ru - sha - la - yim

Gm C F G C Gm A7 Dm F
ya - ha ya - ha tu - li
ya - ha ya - ha tu - li

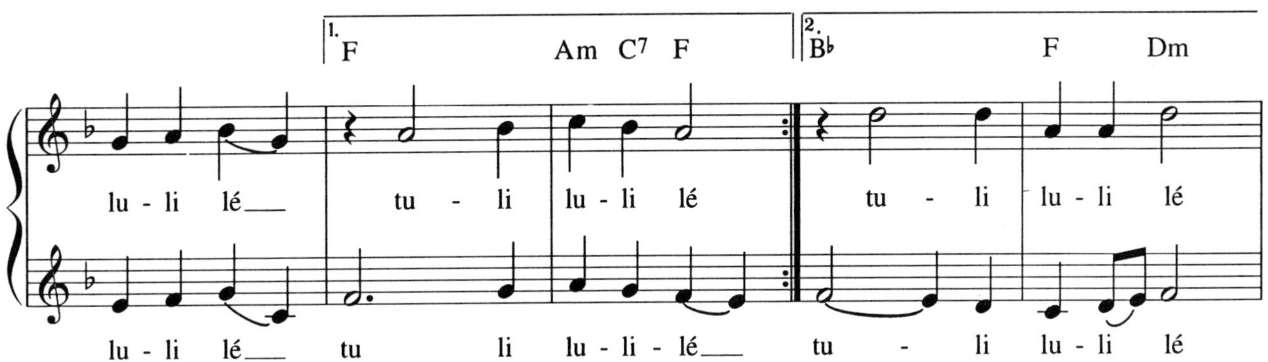

©by the author

Ki mi-tsi-yon té-tsé Torah *Ud-var Ha-shem mi-ru-sha-la-yim*	כִּי מִצִּיּוֹן תֵּצֵא תוֹרָה וּדְבַר ה׳ מִירוּשָׁלָיִם

Truly out of Zion shall come forth the Torah,
and the word of the Lord out of Jerusalem.

Yibane Hamikdash IV

Music: Traditional
Lyrics: Z'mirot Liturgy
Arr: V. Pasternak

Moderately

Dm Gm Dm Dm Gm

Yi - ba - ne ha - mik - dash___ ir Tsi - yon t' - ma -

Dm Dm C Gm F Dm C Gm F Dm C

lé___ v' - sham___ na - shir shir___ cha - dash u - vir - na - na

Dm C7 | F A | F A Dm Am Dm

na - a - le___ yi - le ha - ra - cha - man___

Dm Dm Gm Dm7 Gm Gm

ha - nik - dash___ yit - ba - rach v' - yit - a - le___ al kos___

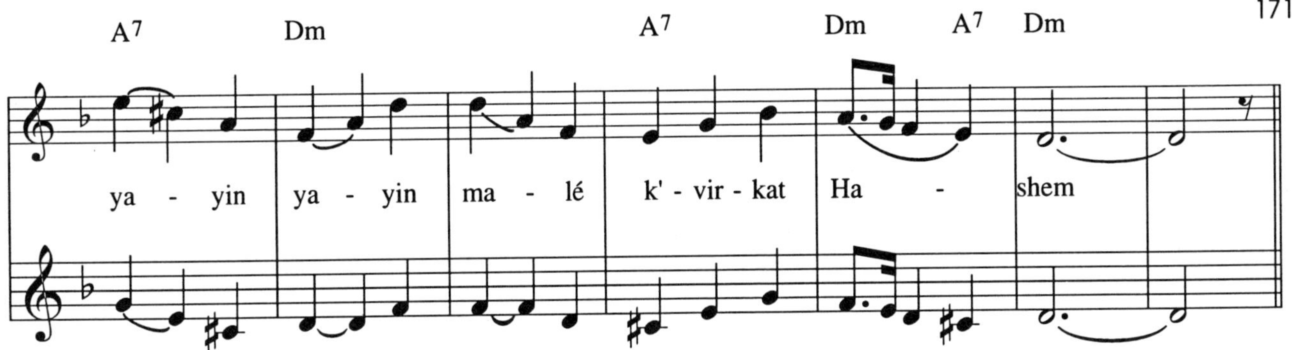

Yi-ba-ne ha-mik-dash ir tsi-yon t'-ma-lé
V'-sham na-shir shir cha-dash
U-vir-na-na na-a-le
Ha-ra-cha-man ha-nik-dash
Yit-ba-rach v'-yit-a-le
Al kos ya-yin ma-lé k'vir-kat Ha-shem

יִבָּנֶה הַמִּקְדָּשׁ עִיר צִיּוֹן תְּמַלֵּא
וְשָׁם נָשִׁיר שִׁיר חָדָשׁ
וּבִרְנָנָה נַעֲלֶה
הָרַחֲמָן הַנִּקְדָּשׁ
יִתְבָּרַךְ וְיִתְעַלֶּה
עַל כּוֹס יַיִן כְּבִרְכַּת ה׳

Let the Temple be restored, Zion refilled, that we may come up singing a new song. Blessed be the Merciful Holy One over a full cup of wine, God's gift.

Yibane Hamikdash V

Music: Traditional
Lyrics: Z'mirot Liturgy

T'fila Lishlom M'dinat Yisraél

Music: D. Burger/M. Lazar
Lyrics: Chief Rabbinate

gén a - lé - ha b'ev- rat chas - de - cha u - f' -
gen b'ev - rat chas - de - cha u - f' -
F/A B/A Em/G A/G D/F♯ D D/C
gen b'ev - rat chas - de - cha u - f' -
ros a - lé - ha suk- kat sh' - lo - me - cha
ros shlo - me - cha u - sh'-lach
Bm Em F Em D4
ros shlo - me - cha u - sh'-lach
o - r' - cha va - a - mit - cha l' - ra -
G C F F B♭/F
o - r' - cha va - a - mit - cha l' - ra -
she - ha sa - re - ha v' - yo - a - tze - ha
F C/E Dm Am/C B♭ Am G
she - ha v' - yo - a - tze - ha
cha - zék et y'-dé m' - gi - né e - retz kod - she -
C F G C G6/B Am F

nu v'-han-chi - lém E - lo - hé - nu y' - shu -
C/E G Am Em/G Dm/F C/E
v'-han-chi - lém E - lo - hé - nu y' - shu -
5
a va - a - te - ret ni - tza-chon ta - at rém
Dm C/E F B♭ F
5
a va - a - te - ret ni - tza-chon ta - at rém
C G B♭ F C G F/G G/C C
v'-na - ta - ta sha - lom sha - lom ba -
G/C C G C G C F G/F
v'-na - ta - ta sha - lom ah
a - retz v'-sim - chat o - lam l'-chol yosh-ve - ha
F C/E Dm Am/C B♭ F/A
ah

A - vi - nu she - ba - sha - ma - yim
G4 C F/C G C G/B
ba -
Am F Dm/C C G6/B Am Em/G
tzur Yis - ra - él v' - go - a - lo ba - réch et m'- di -
rech et m'- di - nat Yis - ra - él re - sheet tzmi-chat re -
F Em F Em Dm
nat Yis - ra - él ba - réch et re - sheet tzmi-chat ré -
sheet tzmi-chat g' - u - la - té - nu
C/E F G A♭ E♭
ah
B♭ F Gm A♭ E♭ B♭ F F/G

©by the authors

A-vi-nu she-ba-sha-ma-yim
Tzur Yis-ra-él v'-go-a-lo
Ba-réch et M'-di-nat Yis-ra-él
Ré-sheet tsmi-chat g'-u-la-té-nu
Ha-gén a-le-ha b'-ev-rat chas-de-cha
U-fros a-lé-ha suk-kat sh'-lo-me-cha
U-sh'-lach or-cha va-a-mit-cha
L'-ra-she-ha sa-re-ha v'-yo-a-tze-ha
Cha-zék et y'-dé m'-gi-né e-retz kod-shé-nu
V'-han-chi-lém E-lo-hé-nu y'-shu-a
Va-a-te-ret ni-tsa-chon t'-at-rém
V'-na-ta-ta sha-lom ba-a-retz
V'-sim-chat o-lam l'-chol yosh-ve-ha
A-men se-la

אָבִינוּ שֶׁבַּשָּׁמַיִם
צוּר יִשְׂרָאֵל וְגוֹאֲלוֹ
בָּרֵךְ אֶת מְדִינַת יִשְׂרָאֵל
רֵאשִׁית צְמִיחַת גְאוּלָּתֵינוּ
הָגֵן אָלֶיהָ בְּאֶבְרַת חַסְדֶּךָ
וּפְרוֹס עָלֶיהָ סֻכַּת שְׁלוֹמֶךָ
וּשְׁלַח אוֹרְךָ וַאֲמִתְּךָ
לְרָאשֶׁיהָ שָׂרֶיהָ וְיוֹעֲצֶיהָ
חַזֵּק אֶת יְדֵי מְגִינֵי אֶרֶץ קָדְשֵׁנוּ
וְהַנְחִילֵם אֱלֹהֵינוּ יְשׁוּעָה
וַעֲטֶרֶת נִצָּחוֹן תְּעַטְּרֵם
וְנָתַתָּ שָׁלוֹם בָּאָרֶץ
וְשִׂמְחַת עוֹלָם לְכָל יוֹשְׁבֶיהָ
אָמֵן סֶלָה

Heavenly Father, Israel's strength and protector, bless the State of Israel. May it represent the beginning of Redemption. Protect her in your mercy and spread over her your mantle of peace. And send your light and truth to her leaders, her ministers and her advisers. Strengthen the hands of the defenders of your holy land. Bestow upon them, O Lord, salvation and the crown of victory and grant peace in the land and everlasting joy to all her inhabitants. Amen

KING DAVID'S TOWER

B'tsét Yisraél

Music: Hassidic
Lyrics: Hallel Liturgy
Arr: V. Pasternak

Moderately

B♭m F B♭m F
B' - tsét___ Yis - ra - él mi - mits - ra - yim l' -

B♭m F E♭m F F7 B♭m
sha - na ha - ba - a bi - ru - sha - la - yim b' - tsét___ Yis - ra - él

F B♭m F7 B♭m F7 B♭m
mi - mits - ra - yim l' - sha - na ha - ba - a bi - ru - sha - la - yim

B'-tsét Yis-ra-él mi-mits-ra-yim
L'-sha-na ha-ba-a bi-ru-sha-la-yim

בְּצֵאת יִשְׂרָאֵל מִמִּצְרָיִם
לַשָּׁנָה הַבָּאָה בִּירוּשָׁלַיִם

Israel went out of Egypt. Next year in Jerusalem!

Mashiach

Music: M. Ben-David, M. Laufer
Lyrics: The Thirteen Principles of Faith

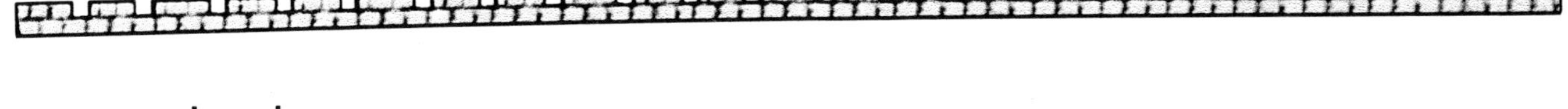

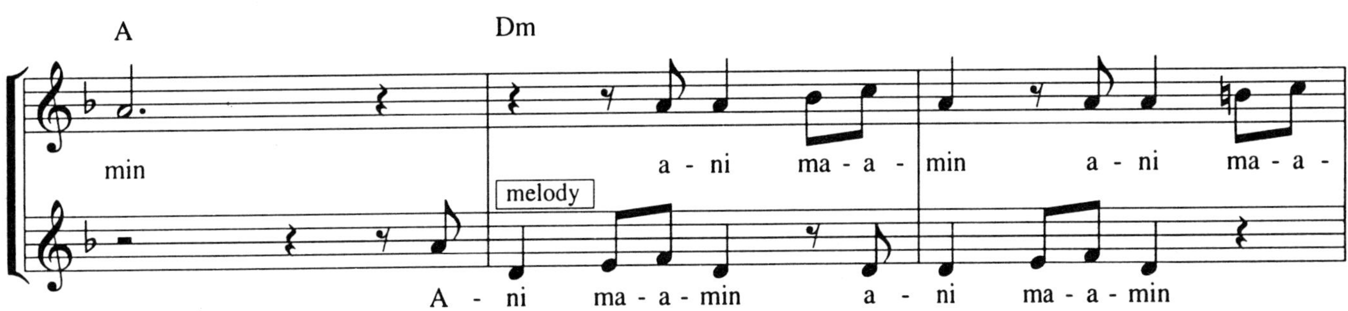

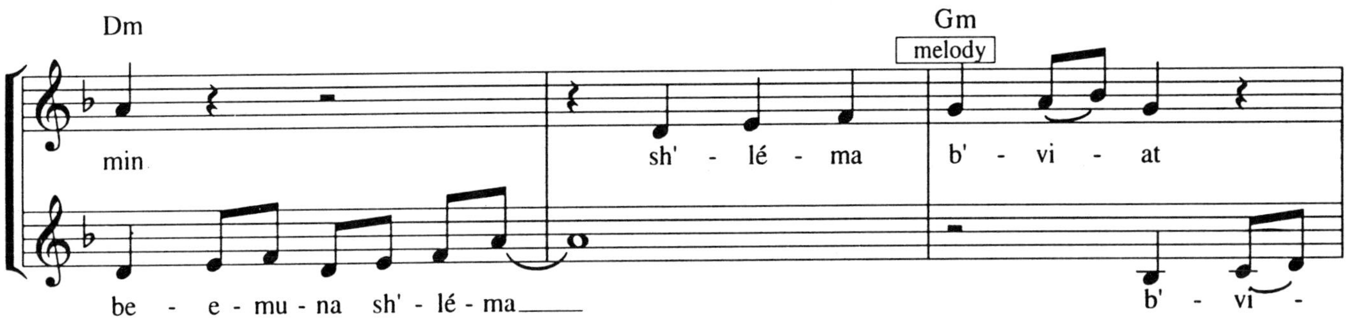

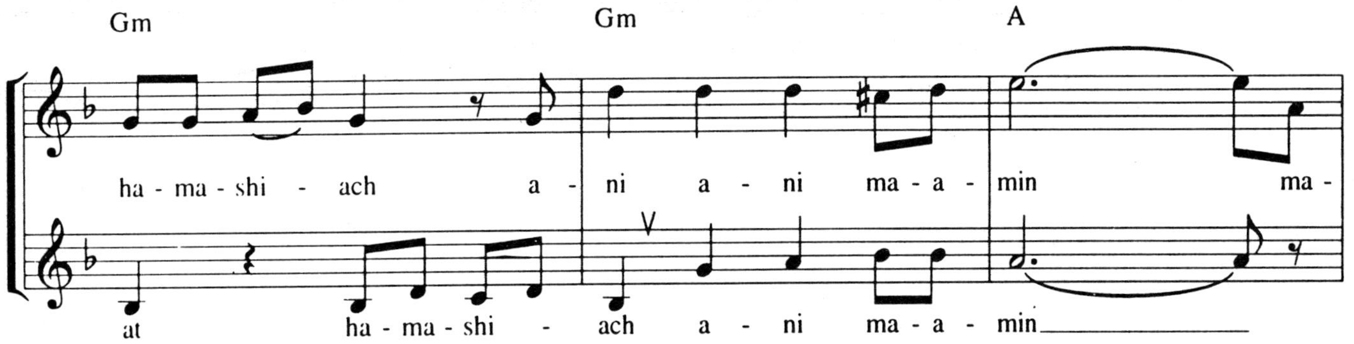

Dm
Gm
shi - ach ma - shi - ach ma - shi - ach
ma -
oy oy oy oy
C
F
shi - ach ma - shi - ach ma - shi - ach
ma -
oy oy oy oy
Dm
Gm
melody
shi - ach ma - shi - ach ma - shi - ach
oy
ma -
ma - shi - ach
melody
oy oy oy oy
C
F
melody
shi - ach ma - shi - ach ma - shi - ach
oy
v' -
ma - shi - ach
oy oy oy oy
v' -
melody
C
af al pi she - yit - ma - mé - a im kol ze a - cha - ke lo a - cha - ke lo b' - chol yom she - ya -
af al pi she - yit - ma - mé - a im kol ze a - cha - ke lo a - cha - ke lo b' - chol yom she - ya -

© by the authors

A-ni ma-a-min be-e-mu-na sh'-lé-ma
B'-vi-at ha-ma-shi-ach
V'-af al pi she-yit-ma-mé-ha
Im kol ze a-cha-ke lo b'-chol yom she-ya-vo

אֲנִי מַאֲמִין בֶּאֱמוּנָה שְׁלֵמָה
בְּבִיאַת הַמָּשִׁיחַ
וְאַף עַל פִּי שֶׁיִּתְמַהְמֵהַּ
עִם כָּל זֶה אֲחַכֶּה לוֹ בְּכָל יוֹם שֶׁיָּבֹא

I believe with perfect faith in the Messiah's coming, even though he may tarry.

N. H. Imber

Dm Gm Dm Gm Dm
Kol__ od ba - lé - vav p' - ni - ma ne - fesh Y' - hu - di

Gm A7 Dm Dm Gm Dm
ho - mi - ya ul' - fa - a - té__ miz - rach ka - di - ma

Gm Dm Gm A7 Dm Dm
a - yin l' - tsi - yon tso - fi - ya od lo av - da

C7 F Dm B♭ C7 F Am Dm
tik - va - té - nu ha - tik - va bat sh'not al - pa - yim li - yot am chof - shi

Gm C7 F Gm A7 Dm Gm A7 Dm
b' - ar - tsé - nu e - rets Tsi - yon Y' - ru - sha - la - yim

Gm Dm C7 F Gm A7 Dm
li - yot am chof - shi b' - ar - tsé - nu e - retz Tsi - yon Y' - ru - sha - la - yim

כָּל עוֹד בַּלֵּבָב פְּנִימָה
נֶפֶשׁ יְהוּדִי הוֹמִיָּה
וּלְפַאֲתֵי מִזְרָח קָדִימָה
עַיִן לְצִיּוֹן צוֹפִיָּה
עוֹד לֹא אָבְדָה תִּקְוָתֵנוּ
הַתִּקְוָה בַּת שְׁנוֹת אַלְפַּיִם
לִהְיוֹת עַם חָפְשִׁי בְּאַרְצֵנוּ
אֶרֶץ צִיּוֹן וִירוּשָׁלָיִם

Kol od ba-lé-vav p'-ni-ma
Nefesh y'-hu-di ho-mi-ya
Ul'-fa-té miz-rach ka-di-ma
A-yin l'-tsi-yon tso-fi-ya
Od lo av-da tik-va-té-nu
Ha-tik-va bat sh'-not al-pa-yim
Li-yot am chof-shi b'-ar-tsé-nu
Erets Tsi-yon vi-ru-sha-la-yim

As long as a Jewish heart beats, and as long as Jewish eyes look eastward, then our two thousand year hope to be a free nation in Zion is not dead.

ANNOTATIONS

B'NÉ VÉTCHA Page 149
From the pen of Cantor Israel Fuchs of Detroit, Michigan. The song was first introduced at an Israeli Hassidic Song Festival and has become popular both there and in the United States.

HAKOTEL Page 139
When the Western Wall, sacred to Judaism since ancient times, was recaptured in 1967 and placed once again in Jewish hands, Dov Seltzer's moving song was heard throughout the land and abroad.

HATIKVAH Page 182
Written in 1878, Hatikvah was formally declared the Zionist anthem during the 18th Zionist Congress in Prague, 1933. At the Declaration of the State of Israel on May 14, 1948, it was sung by the assembly during the opening ceremony and played by members of the Palestine Symphony Orchestra at its conclusion. Both the melody and words have been slightly altered since the establishment of the State of Israel. The version presented here is the official version.

KI MITSIYON Page 168
Written by Emanuel Pugatchev (Amiran) this is one of the truly durable songs of Israel. The song with its text from the liturgy is often found in the concert repertoire of both amateur and professional choruses.

L'MA'AN TSIYON Page 130
The melody set to a text from Isaiah was given its first performance at the Yom Y'rushalayim Festival (The Jerusalem Day Festival) held in a Jerusalem amphitheater in 1970.

L'SHANA HABA'A Page 72
For centuries Jews have concluded the Passover Seder with the words *l'shana haba'a birushalayim* , next year in Jerusalem. With the Old City of Jerusalem returned to Israel in 1967 the word *habnuya* (the rebuilt) has been added to the end of the phrase.

LACH Y'RUSHALAYIM Page 11
This song appeared after the Six Day War and its spirited lilt reflected the new and proud feelings with regard to a returned Jerusalem.

SHALOM SHUVCHA HAKOTEL Page 131
This stirring and highly emotional song was written in the United states by Chaim Najman, based on a poem by Elchanan Indelman, in the aftermath of the Six Day War.

SHEYIBANE BÉT HAMIKDASH Page 88
The melody is the closing section of a well known cantorial composition. It became closely associated with the late cantor Moshe Koussevitsky. This song has remained a favorite composition in the cantorial repertoire.

SHEYIBANE BÉT HAMIKDASH II Page 146
Written by Motti Giladi, a well-known Israeli singer-entertainer, this song has three distinct moods—the first is in a rock tempo, the second is Oriental in feeling and the third is typically Hassidic.

SIMCHU ET Y'RUSHALAYIM Page 57
has been credited to Rabbi Yeshaya Shapiro, who was known in Israell as *"Ha-admor Hachaluts,"* the Pioneer Rebbe. This song is often thought to be an Israeli Folk melody.

SISU ET Y'RUSHALAYIM Page 122
Sisu Et Y'rushalayim entered the Israeli musical scene via a Hassidic Song Festival. With text based on a number of different verses in Isaiah, Akiva Nof has fashioned a song which has proved durable. It is popular in many areas where Jews reside.

T'FILA LISHLOM HAM'DINA- PRAYER FOR THE PEACE OF ISRAEL Page 172
This modern prayer composed after the birth of Israel in 1948, is recited in synagogues throughout the world during services on Sabbath and Festival mornings.

TÉN SHABBAT Page 156
This was the featured song in an Israeli produced movie *Ani Y'rushalmi*—I am from Jerusalem—with Yehoram Gaon. It became extremely popular especially in rock tempo

UVA'U HA'OVDIM Page 56
One of the most enduring melodies of the late Rabbi Shlomo Carlebach. It is often referred to by the title "Birushalayim".

Y'RUSHALAYIM Page 98
This well known song has a permanent place in the repertoire of Israeli song. Although the authorship of the melody is not known, Avigdor Hameiri's words directed to the city of Jerusalem have made it a long standing favorite.

JERUSALEM OF GOLD- Y'RUSHALAYIM SHEL ZAHAV Page 94
Without doubt this was the most important and widely heard song in the immediate aftermath of the Six Day War in 1967. It was introduced at the yearly Song Festival presented as the climax to Israel Independence Day and was sung by Shuli Natan. With the retaking of the old city of Jersualem and the return of the sacred Western Wall, the song assumed additional emotional appeal. Within a period of days following the Six Day War the song was recorded by a number of artists both in Israel and in the United States. The song became known throughout the world wherever Jews reside.

Y'VARECH'CHA Page 115
A prize winning song presented at the 1970 Israeli Chassidic Song Festival. *Y'varech'cha* has proved its staying power and is still very popular today.

JERUSALEM IS MINE Page 20
One of the most enduring Jerusalem songs of the late 20th century, from the pen of Kenny Karen, noted song writer and composer of advertising commercials.

Al Kapav Yavi Page 38

Bi-ru-sha-la-yim yesh-no	בִּירוּשָׁלַיִם יֶשְׁנוֹ
Ish l'-gam-ri lo tsa-ir	אִישׁ לְגַמְרֵי לֹא צָעִיר
She-ba-na har-bé ba-tim	שֶׁבָּנָה הַרְבֵּה בָּתִּים
B'-chol pi-not ha-ir	בְּכָל פִּנּוֹת הָעִיר
Hu ma-kir kol sim-ta	הוּא מַכִּיר כָּל סִמְטָה
Kol r'-chov u-sh'-chu-na	כָּל רְחוֹב וּשְׁכוּנָה
Hu bo-ne et ha-ir	הוּא בּוֹנֶה אֶת הָעִיר
K'-var shiv-im sha-na	כְּבָר שִׁבְעִים שָׁנָה
V'-hu cho-lém ki ch'-mo she-et ha-ir ba-na	וְהוּא חוֹלֵם כִּי כְמוֹ שֶׁאֶת הָעִיר בָּנָה
Ya-ni-ach la-mik-dash et e-ven ha-pi-na	יָנִיחַ לַמִּקְדָּשׁ אֶת אֶבֶן הַפִּנָּה
Al ka-pav o-to ya-vi	עַל כַּפָּיו אוֹתוֹ יָבִיא
L'-é-li-ya-hu ha-na-vi	לְאֵלִיָּהוּ הַנָּבִיא

Shiro Shel Aba Page 23

Im ba-har na-ta-ta e-rez, e-rez bim-kom dar-dar	אִם בָּהָר נָטַעְתָּ אֶרֶז, אֶרֶז בִּמְקוֹם דַּרְדַּר
Ba-har na-ta-ta e-rez, e-rez bim-kom dar-dar	בָּהָר נָטַעְתָּ אֶרֶז, אֶרֶז בִּמְקוֹם דַּרְדַּר
Lo la-shav a-chi na-ta-ta bim-kom dar-dar	לֹא לַשָּׁוְא אַחִי נָטַעְתָּ בִּמְקוֹם דַּרְדַּר
Ki min ha-a-ra-zim ha-é-lu yi-ba-ne ha-mik-dash	כִּי מִן הָאֲרָזִים הָאֵלוּ יִבָּנֶה הַמִּקְדָּשׁ

Im lo shar-ta li shir a-da-yin	אִם לֹא שַׁרְתָּ לִי שִׁיר עֲדַיִן
Shi-ra li miz-mor cha-dash	שִׁירָה לִי מִזְמוֹר חָדָשׁ
She-hu a-tik mi-ya-yin u-ma-tok mi-d'-vash	שֶׁהוּא עַתִּיק מִיַּיִן וּמָתוֹק מִדְּבָשׁ
Shir she-hu k'-ven al-pa-yim u-v'-chol yom cha-dash	שִׁיר שֶׁהוּא כְּבֶן אַלְפַּיִם וּבְכָל יוֹם חָדָשׁ

Sisu Et Y'rushalayim Page 122

Al ti-ra v'-al té-chat av-di Ya-a-kov	אַל תִּירָא וְאַל תֵּחַת עַבְדִּי יַעֲקֹב
Ki ya-fu-tsu m'-san-e-cha Sisu.......	כִּי יָפוּצוּ מְשַׂנְאֶיךָ מִפָּנֶיךָ שִׂישׂוּ ....

S'-i sa-viv é-na-yich u-r'-i ku-lam	שְׂאִי סָבִיב עֵינַיִךְ וּרְאִי כֻּלָּם
Nik-b'-tsu u-va-u lach Sisu.......	נִקְבְּצוּ וּבָאוּ לָךְ שִׂישׂוּ ....

V'-a-méch a-méch ku-lam tsa-di-kim	וְעַמֵּךְ עַמֵּךְ כֻּלָּם צַדִּיקִים
L'-o-lam yir-shu a-rets Sisu.......	לְעוֹלָם יִירְשׁוּ אָרֶץ שִׂישׂוּ ....

INDEX OF FIRST LINES

ALPHABETICAL INDEX

BJE/RMC
008717